Aylmer Ontario Book 1 in Colour Photos, Saving Our History One Photo at a Time

Photography
by Barbara Raué
2014

Series Name:
Cruising Ontario

Book 78: Aylmer Book 1

Cover photo: 20 South Street

Series Name: Cruising Ontario
Saving Our History One Photo at a Time

Book 33: Southampton
Book 34: Jarvis
Book 35: Hagersville
Book 36: Caledonia
Book 37: Simcoe
Book 38: Cambridge
Part 1 – Galt Book 1
Book 39: Cambridge
Part 1 – Galt Book 2
Book 40: Cambridge
Part 2 – Preston
Book 41: Cambridge
Part 3 – Hespeler
Book 42: Kitchener 1
Book 43: Kitchener 2
Book 46: Shelburne
Book 47: Alton, Mono
Book 48: London Colour
Book 49: St. Thomas
Book 50: Orangeville 1
Book 51: Orangeville 2
Book 52: Orangeville 3
Book 53: Dundas 1
Book 54: Dundas 2
Book 55: Dundas 3
Book 56: Stratford
Book 57: Hanover
Book 58: NewHamburg1
Book 59: NewHamburg2

Book 60: Waterdown
Book 61: Burlington
Book 62: Stoney Creek
Book 63: Seaforth
Book 64: Aberfoyle, Morriston and Rockton
Book 65: Eden Mills
Book 66: Ancaster and Mount Hope
Book 67: Jarvis,Pt.Dover
Book 68: Fergus, Elora
Book 69: Elora
Book 70: Elmira Book 1
Book 71: Elmira 2 & Area
Book72:St.Jacobs, St.Clements, Heidelberg,Crosshill,Bamberg
Book 73: Linwood, Macton
Book 74: Wellesley
Book 75: Listowel
Book 76: Palmerston
Book 77:Dorchester to Aylmer
Book 78: Aylmer 1
Book 79: Aylmer 2

Other Books by Barbara Raue

Coins of Gold

Arrows, Indians and Love

The Life and Times of Barbara
Volume 1: Inventions That Have Enhanced My Life
Volume 2: Entertainment That I Have Enjoyed
Volume 3: East Coast Trips
Volume 4: Olympics Have Always Intrigued Me
Volume 5: Wonders of the World
Volume 6: Caribbean Cruises We Have Enjoyed
Volume 7: Animals
Volume 8: Storms and Other Major Disasters in My Lifetime
Volume 9: Wars, Terrorist Attacks and Major Disasters

The Cromwell Family Book

Laura Secord Discovered

Visit Barbara's website to view all of her books
http://barbararaue.ca

Aylmer

Aylmer is located in southern Ontario just north of Lake Erie on Catfish Creek. It is 20 kilometers south of Highway 401. It is located on Highway 3 between St. Thomas to the west, and Tillsonburg to the east.

In October 1817, John Van Patter, an emigrant from New York State, obtained 200 acres of land and was the first settler on the site of Aylmer. During the 1830s a general store was opened and village lots sold.

Originally called Troy, in 1835 it was renamed Aylmer after Lord Aylmer, then Governor-in-Chief of British North America. By 1851 local enterprises included sawmills and flour-mills powered by water from Catfish Creek.

By the mid-1860s Aylmer, with easy access to Lake Erie, became the marketing centre for a rich agricultural and timber producing area. Aylmer benefited greatly from the construction of the 145-mile Canada Air Line Railway from Glencoe to Fort Erie.

The coming of the Great Western Air Line railway in 1873 encouraged manufacturing and mills, a foundry, a pork-packing house, a milk-evaporating plant, and shoe factory were among the main establishments. An Airfield for training was established nearby in World War 2 which became the nucleus of the Ontario Police College.

The Aylmer Canning Factory was established in 1879; it packed peas, beans, cider, pickles, vinegar, sauces, meats and fruits.

Imperial Tobacco Canada built a plant in 1945. At its peak, it employed more than 600 full-time and seasonal workers. In its prime, the plant could store 110 million tons of tobacco and had an October to April production capacity of 100 million tons. Of this, 20 to 25 million tons were for export to other countries, making it one of Canada's leading exporters. The rest of the processed tobacco was shipped to Imperial's cigarette production plant in Guelph. After declining tobacco sales in Canada, Imperial began downsizing in the 1990s and closed in 2007.

Table of Contents

Talbot Street West	Page 6
St. George Street	Page 15
Rutherford Avenue	Page 17
South Street	Page 19
Harvey Street	Page 34
Forest Street	Page 42
Clarence Street	Page 43
John Street South	Page 44
King Street	Page 57
Maple Street	Page 59
Chestnut Street	Page 60
Oak Street	Page 61
Cedar Street	Page 64
Architectural Terms	Page 65
Building Styles	Page 69

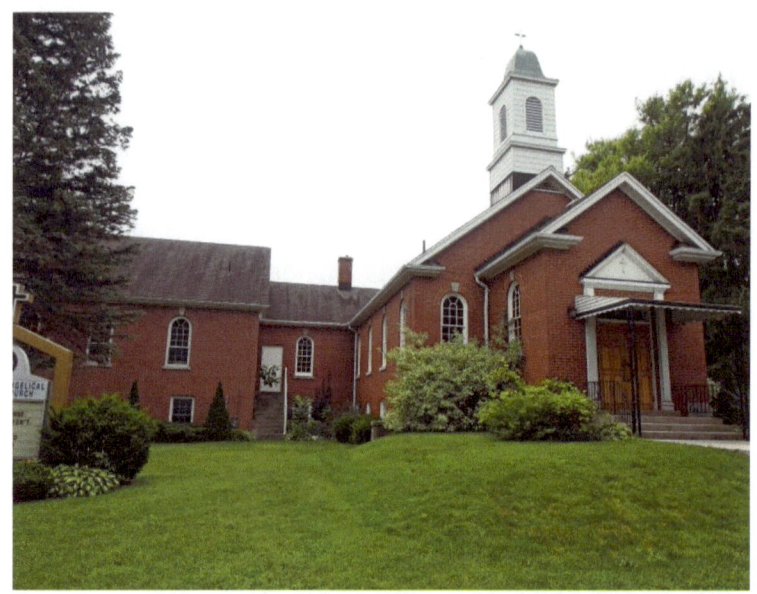

Talbot Street West - St. John's Evangelical Lutheran Church
c. 1952, cornice return on gable

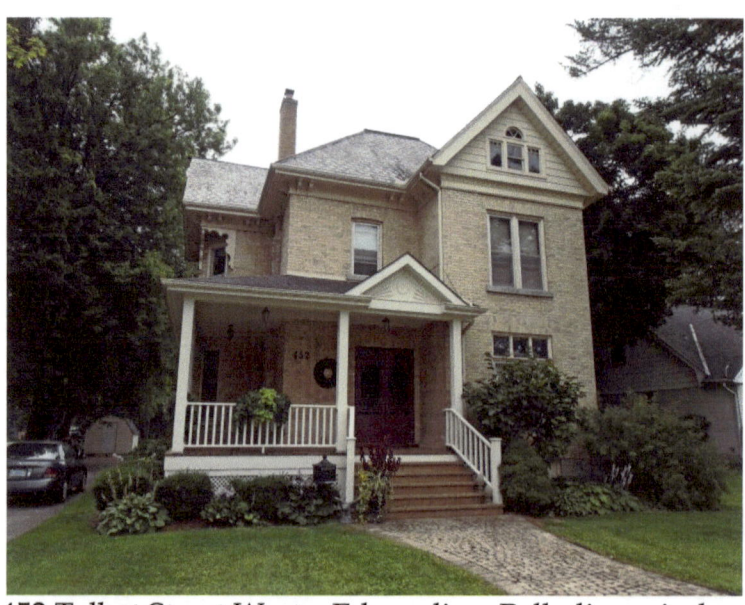

452 Talbot Street West – Edwardian, Palladian window

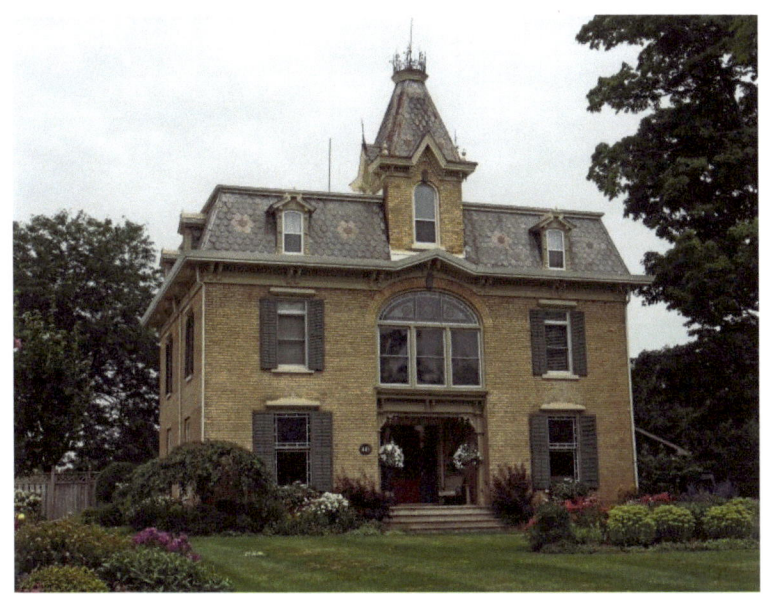

445 Talbot Street West – Second Empire style, mansard roof,
Iron cresting, window hoods on dormers

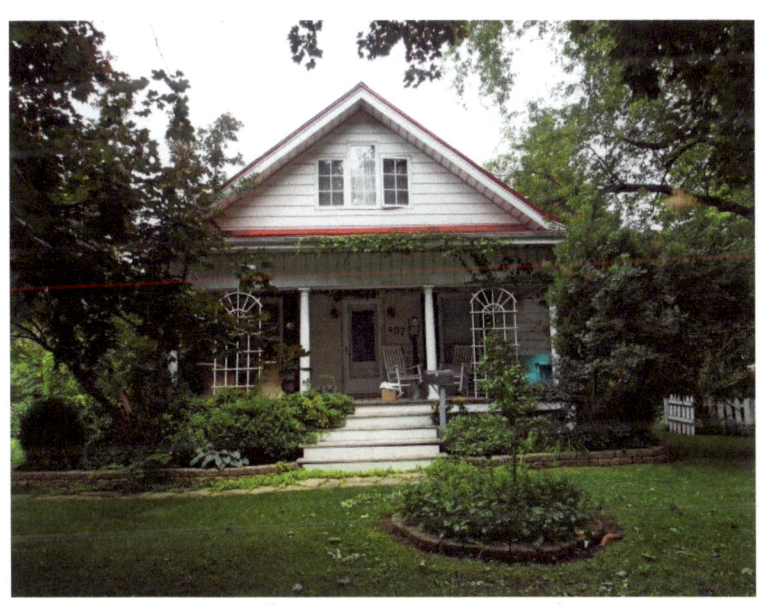

407 Talbot Street West - Gothic

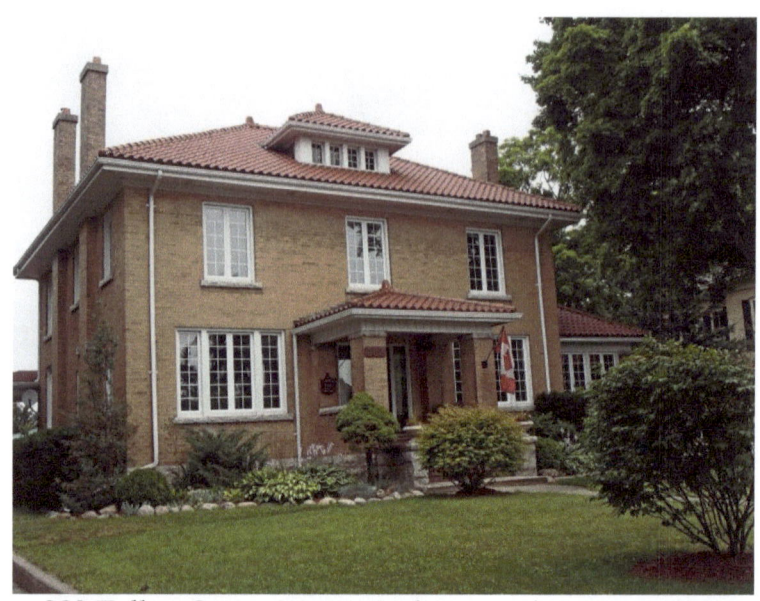

383 Talbot Street West – Italianate, dormer in attic
Hipped roof

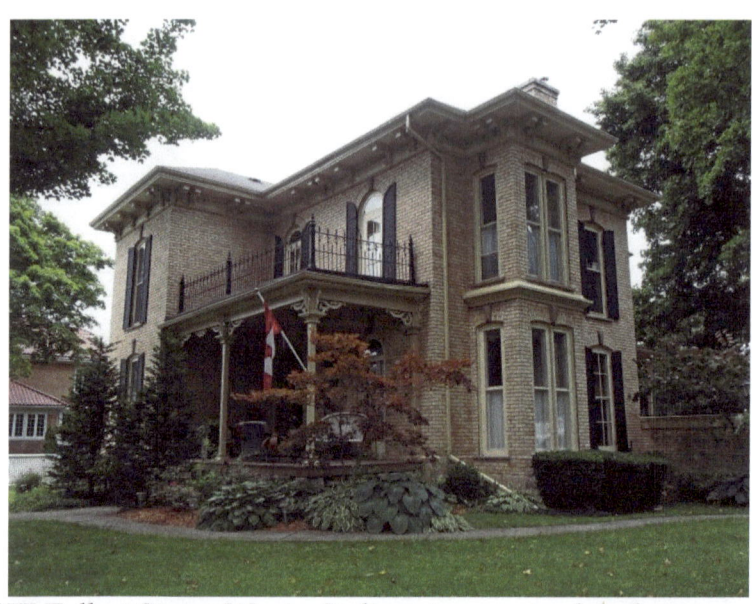

375 Talbot Street West – Italianate, cornice brackets, two-storey tower-like bays, balcony on second floor

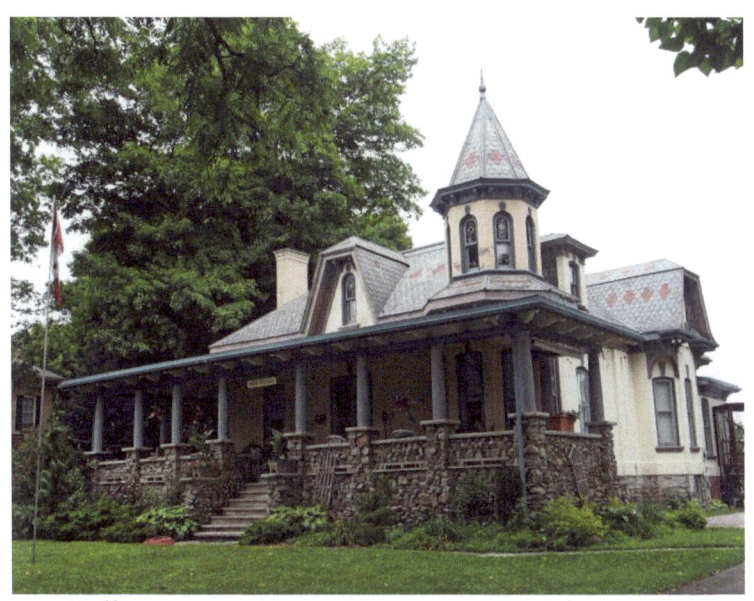

Talbot Street West – Queen Anne style, turret, trichromatic tile work

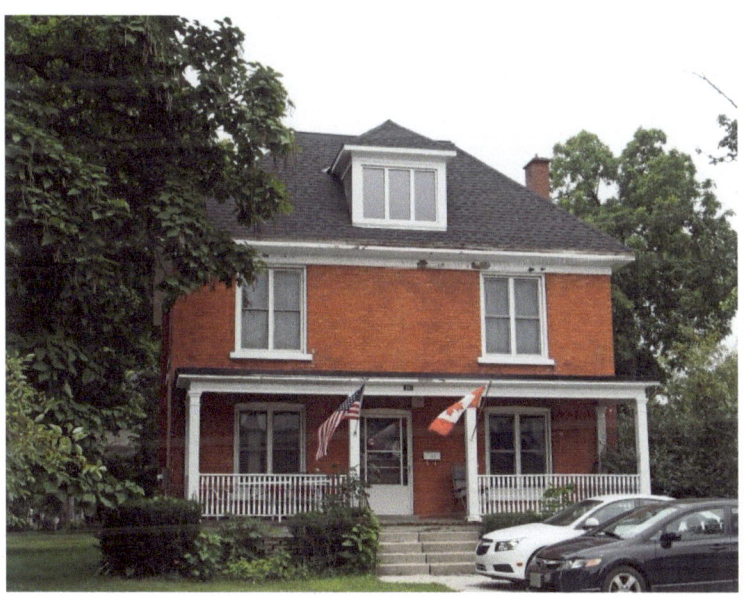

361 Talbot Street West – Italianate, hipped roof, dormer in attic

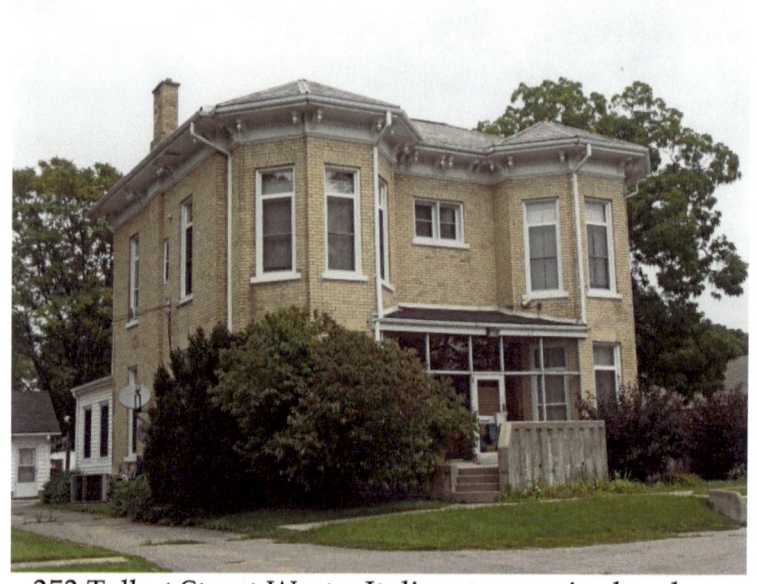

353 Talbot Street West – Italianate, cornice brackets
Two-storey tower-like bays

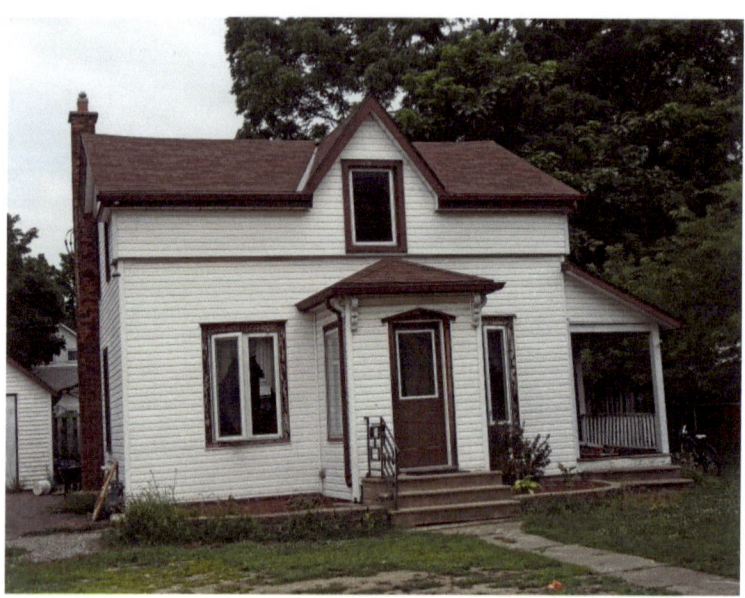

Talbot Street West - Gothic

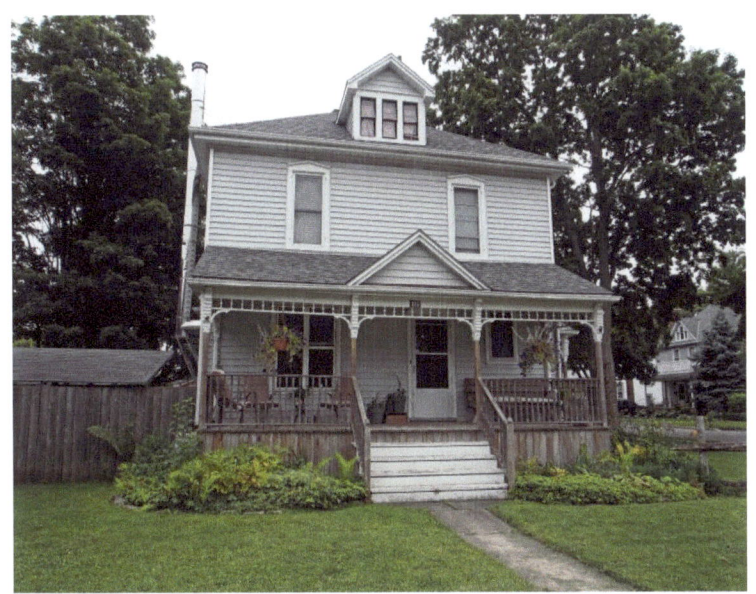

326 Talbot Street West - dormer

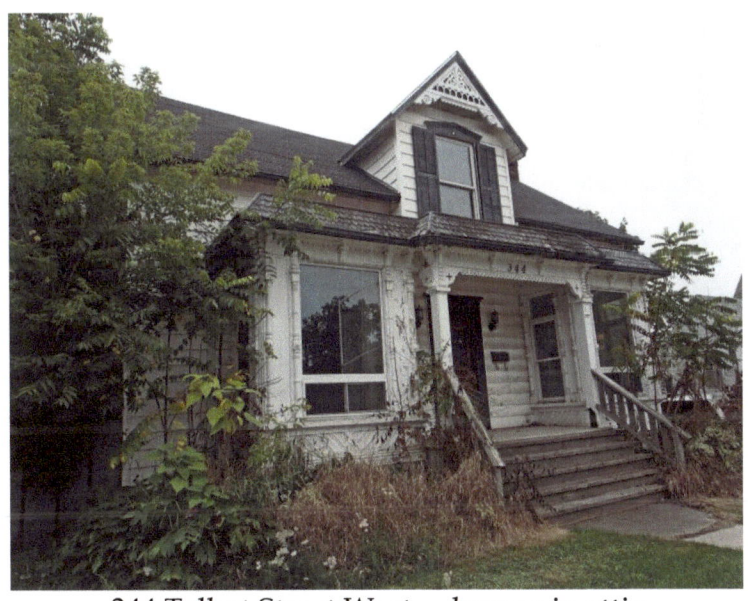

344 Talbot Street West – dormer in attic

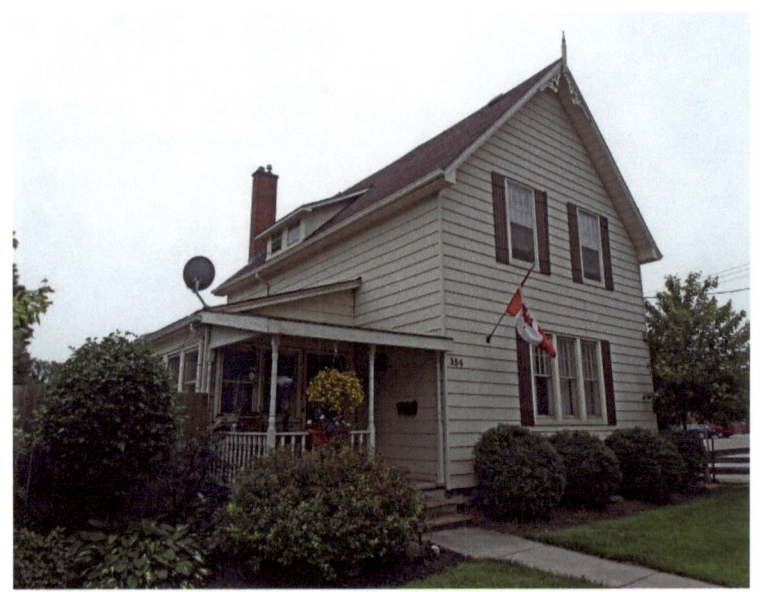

354 Talbot Street West – Gothic Revival

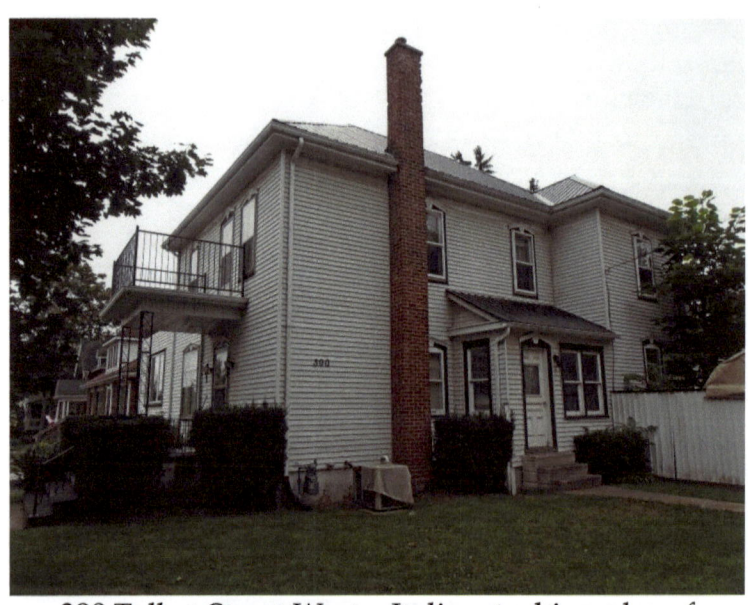

390 Talbot Street West – Italianate, hipped roof

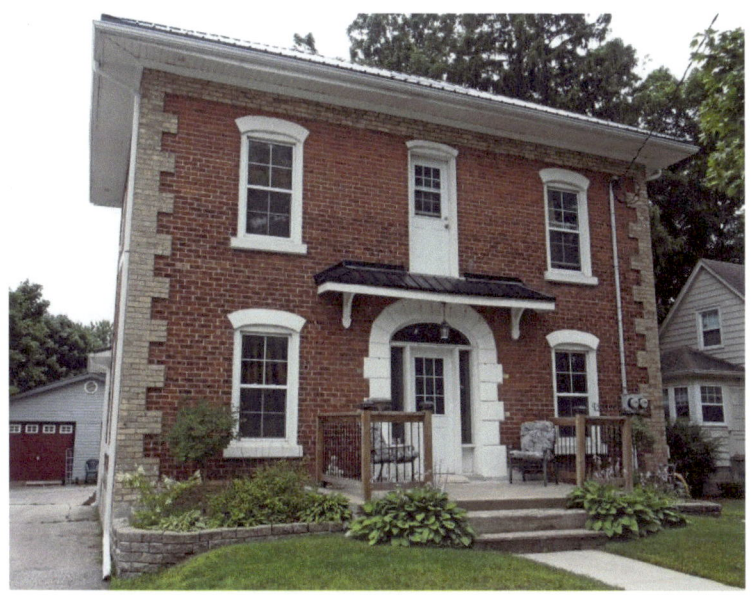

Talbot Street West – Italianate, corner quoins

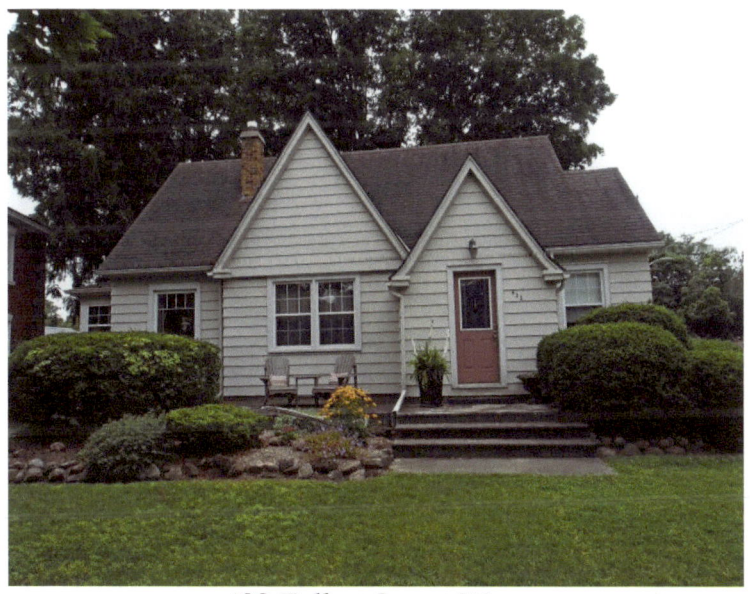

432 Talbot Street West

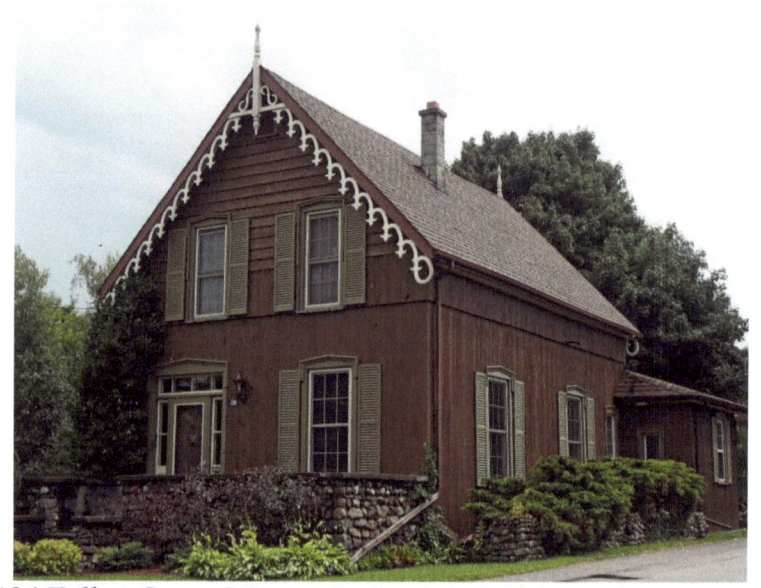

136 Talbot Street West – Gothic Revival, Vergeboard trim
with finial on gable

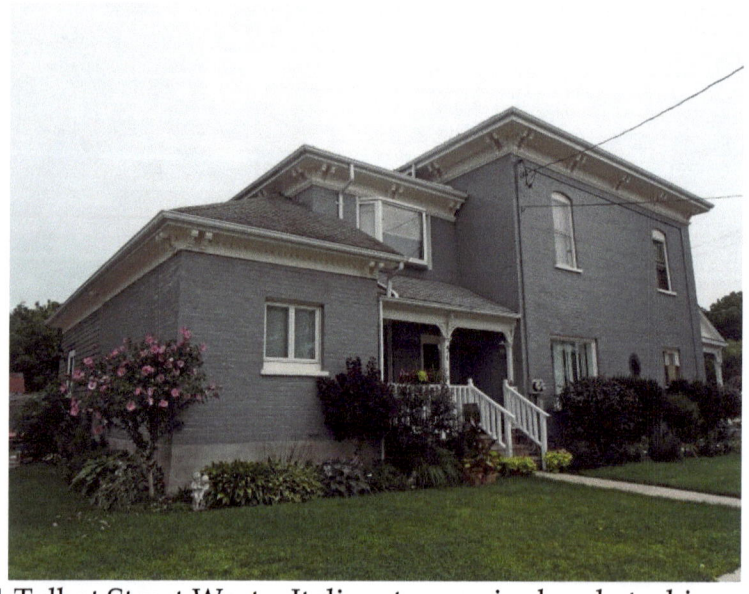

51 Talbot Street West – Italianate, cornice brackets, hip roof

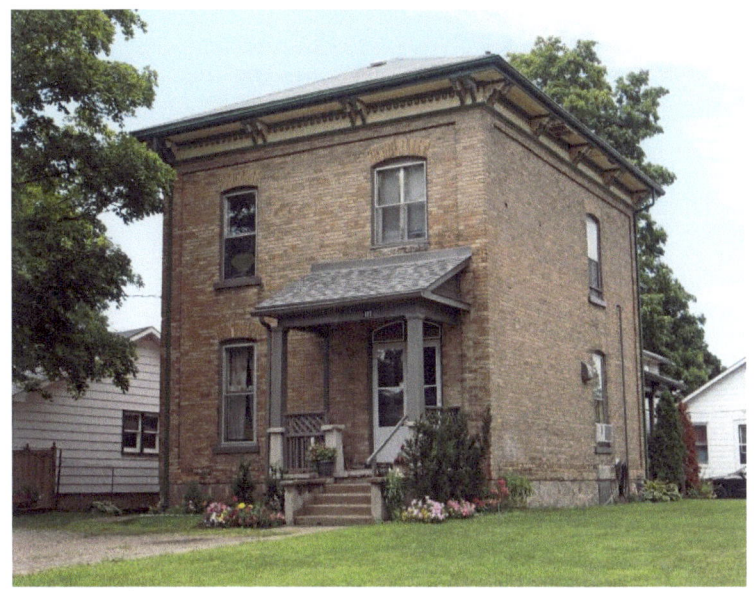

127 Talbot Street West – Italianate, cornice brackets, decorative cornice

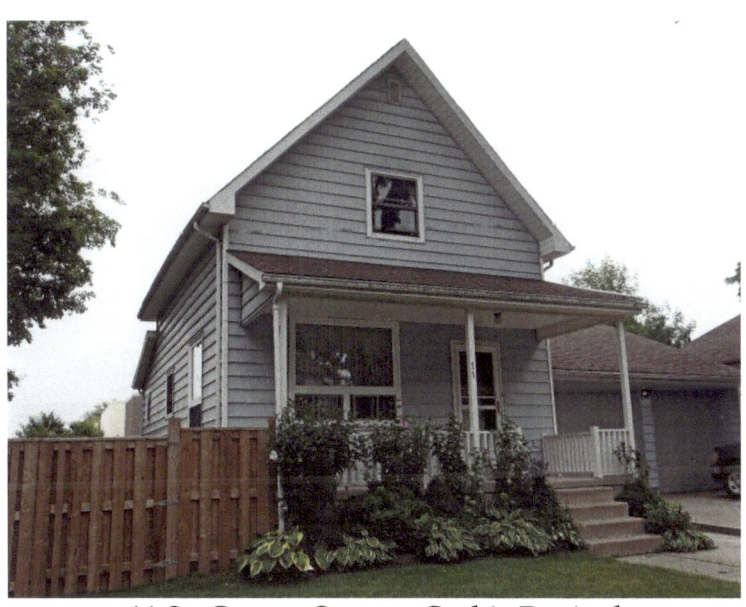

11 St. George Street – Gothic Revival

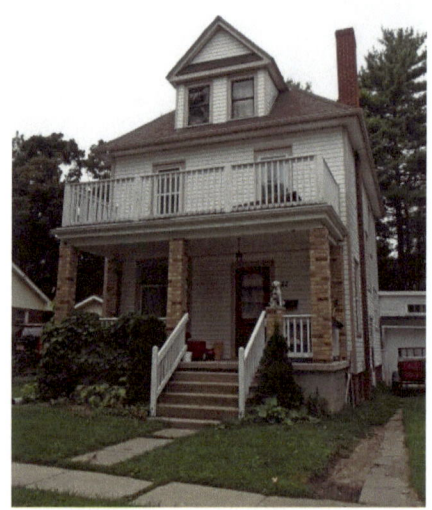

12 St. George Street – Italianate, dormer in attic, balcony on second floor

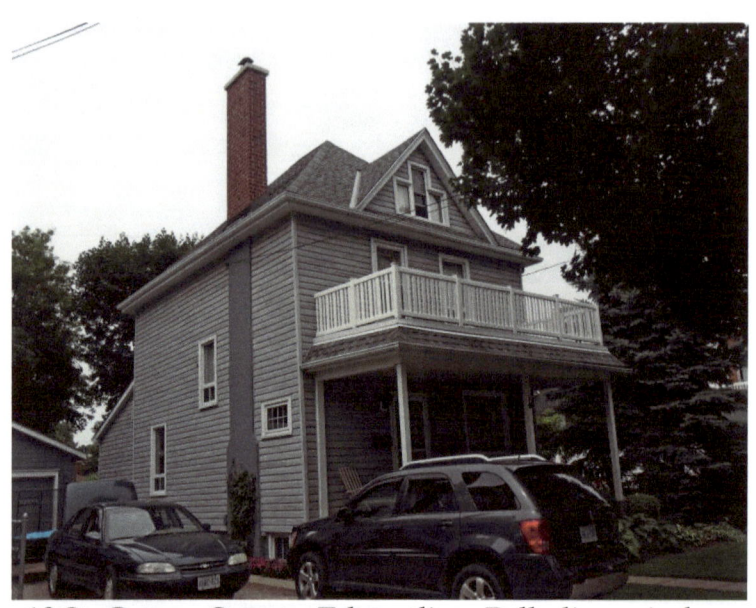

10 St. George Street – Edwardian, Palladian window

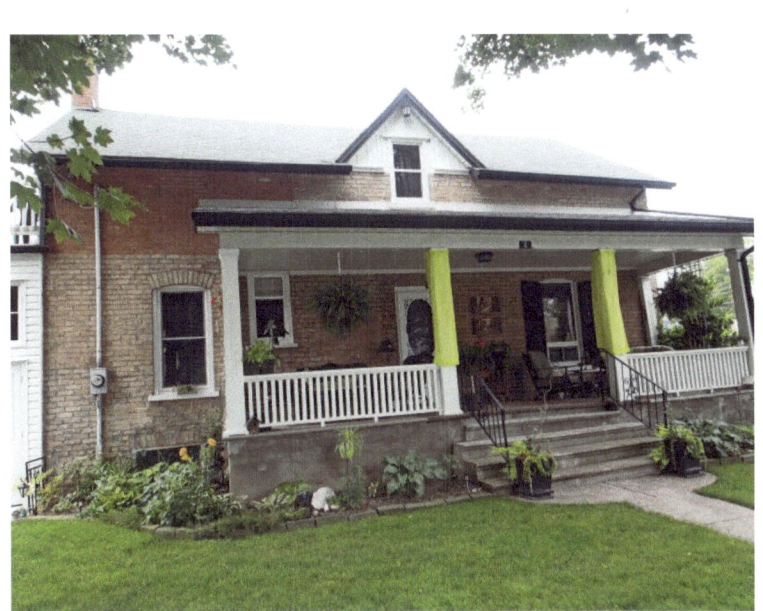

2 St. George Street – Gothic cottage

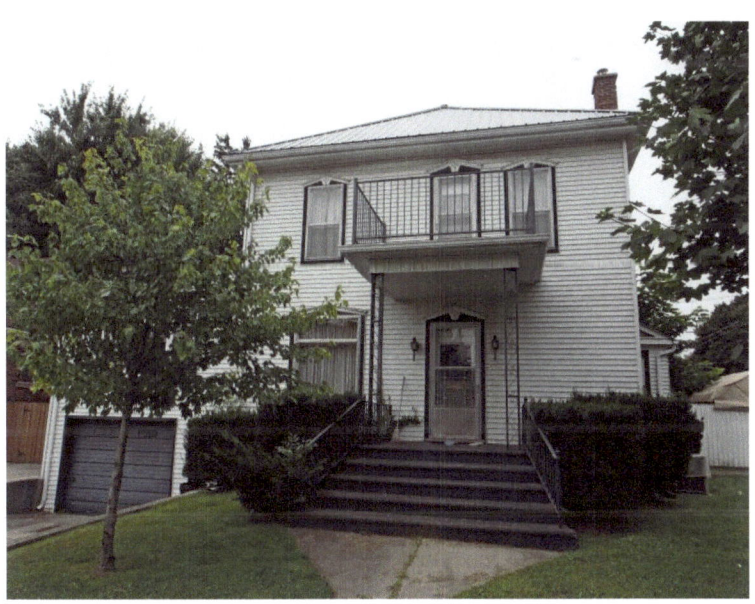

Rutherford Avenue – Italianate, hip roof,
second floor balcony

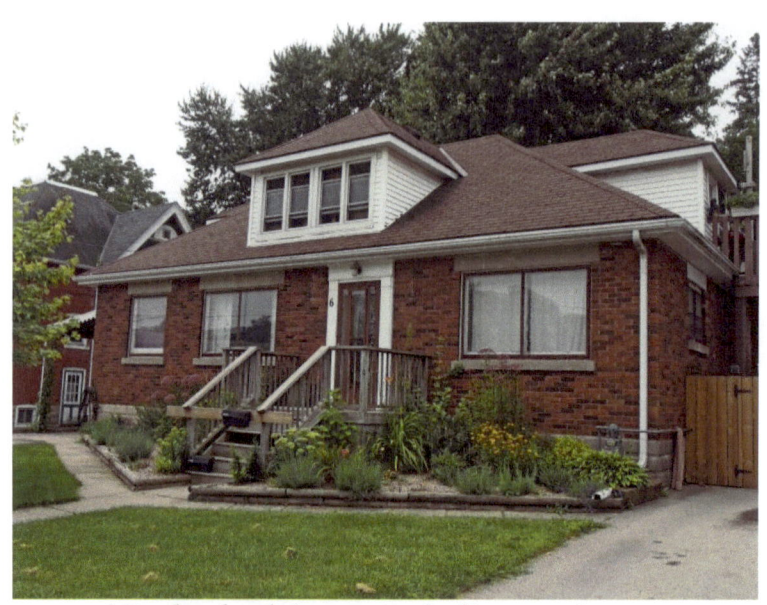

6 Rutherford Avenue – Italianate, dormer

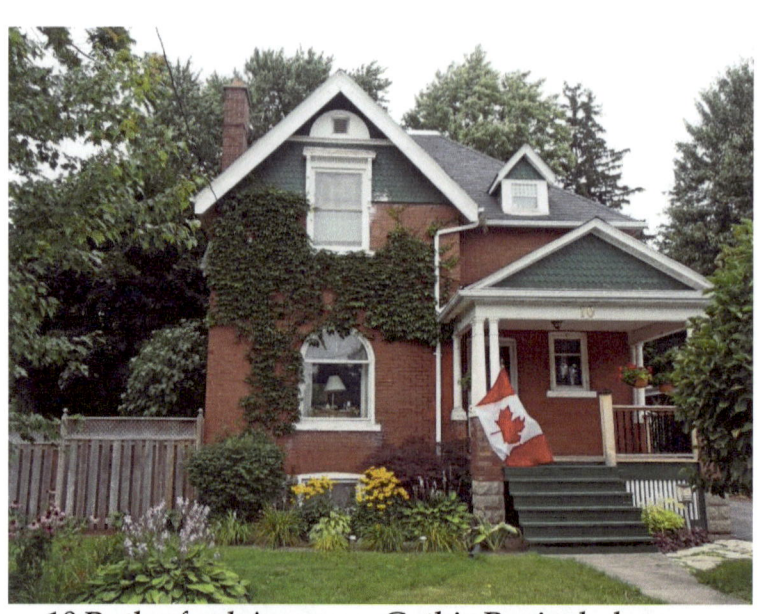

10 Rutherford Avenue – Gothic Revival, dormer,
pediment, window hoods

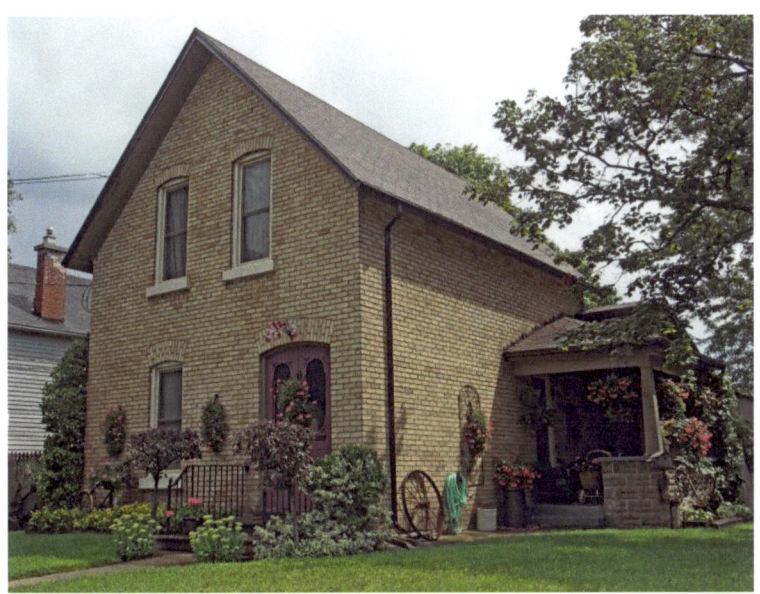

88 South Street – Gothic Revival

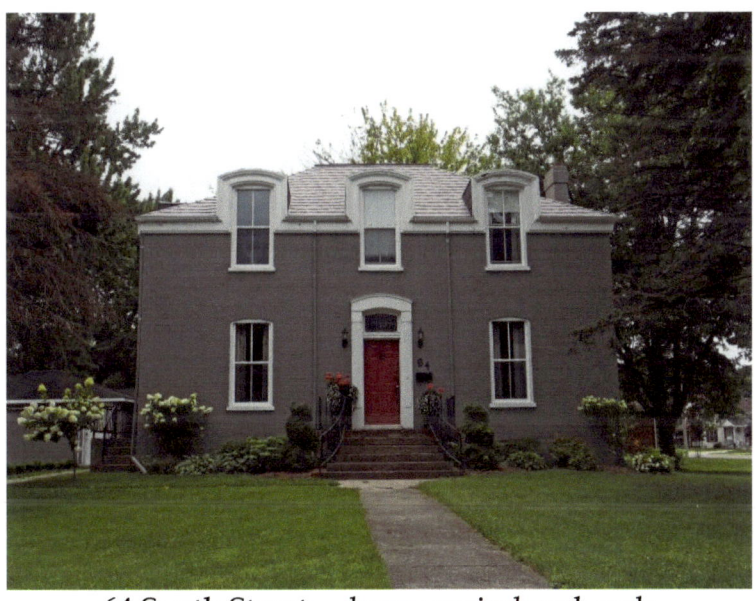

64 South Street – dormer window hoods

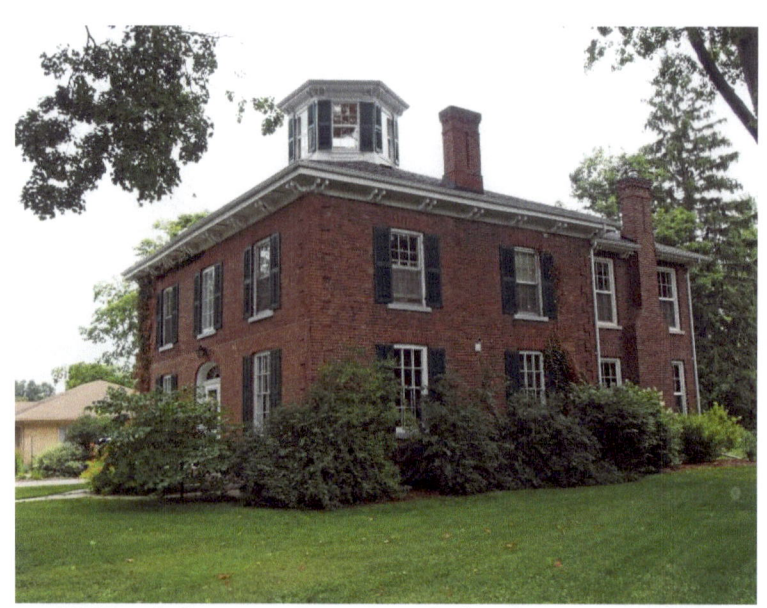

30 South Street – Georgian, belvedere on rooftop

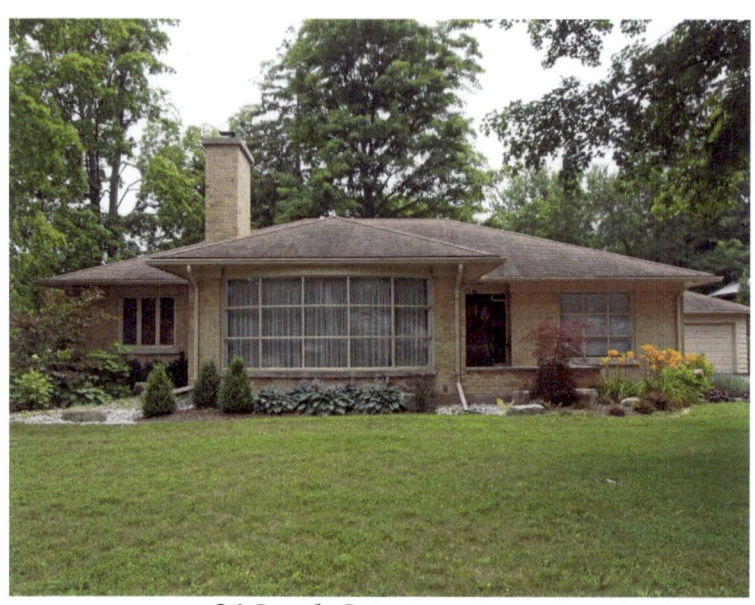

26 South Street - cottage

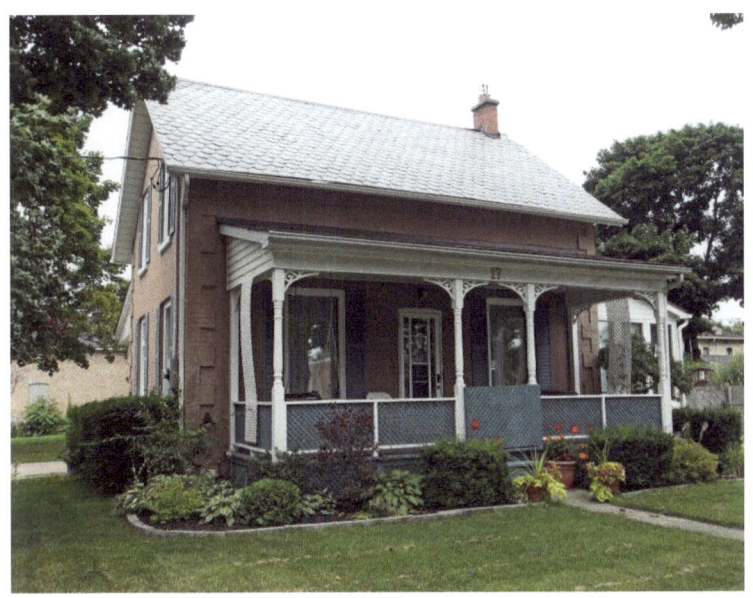

17 South Street – Gothic Revival

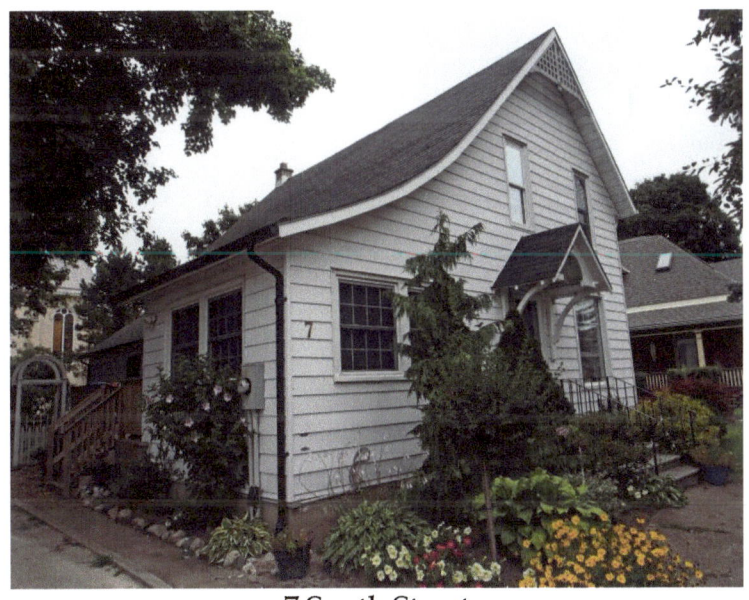

7 South Street

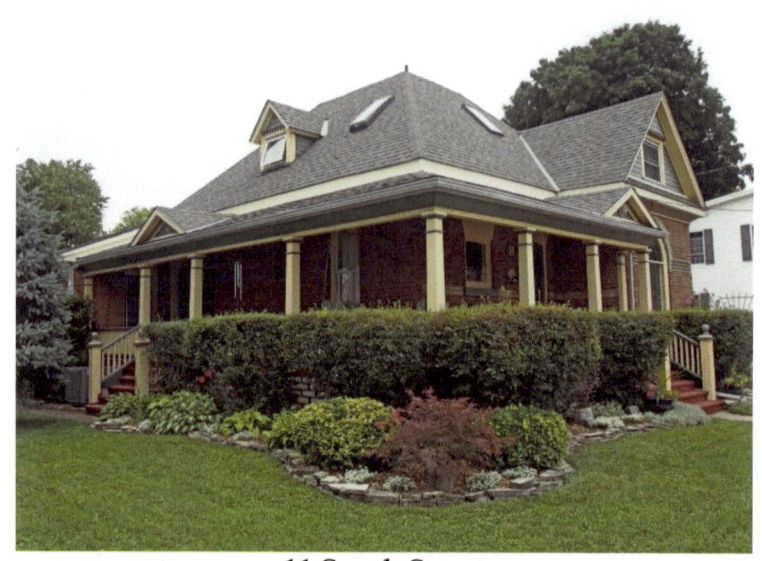

11 South Street

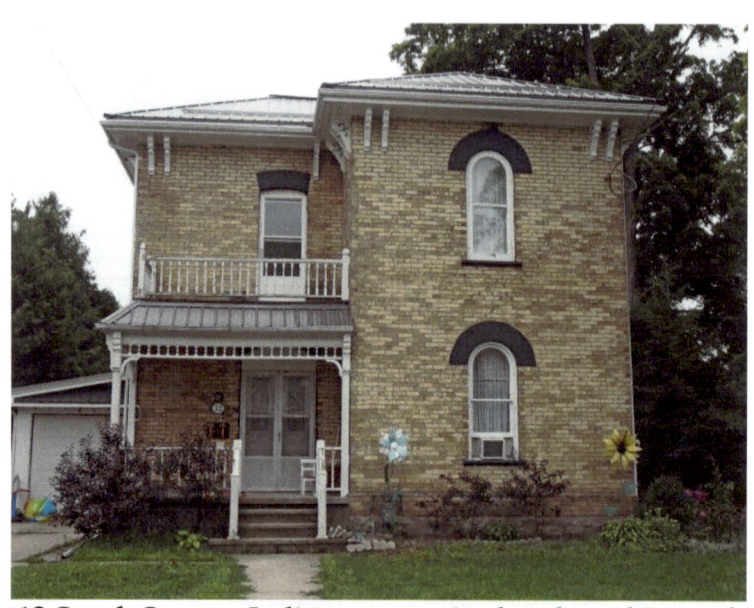

12 South Street – Italianate, cornice brackets, hip roof, Romanesque style window arches, balcony on second floor

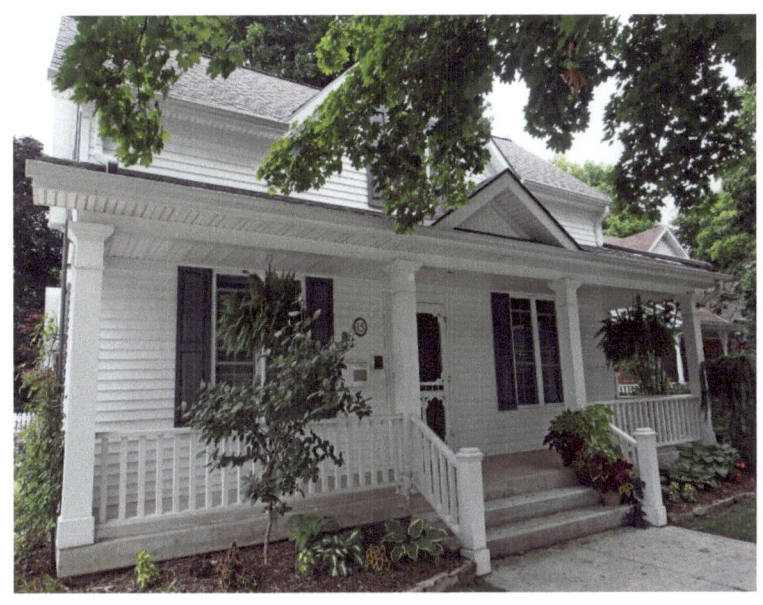

15 South Street – Gothic Revival

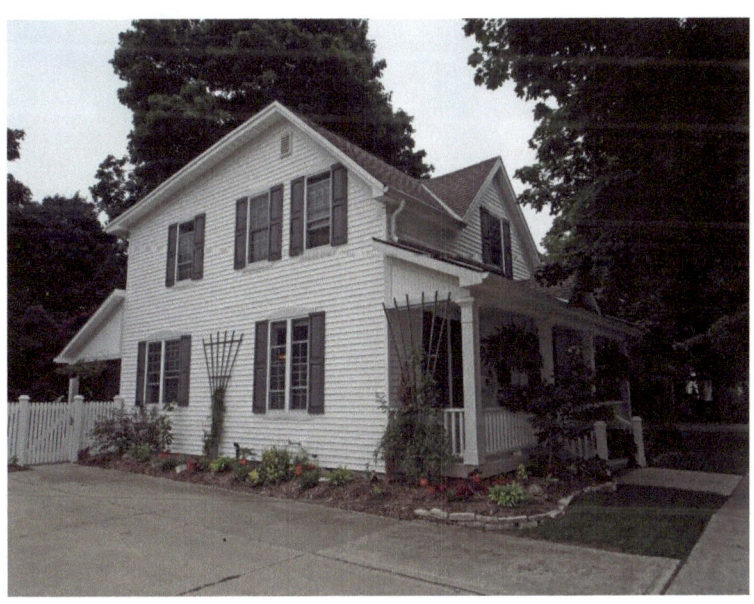

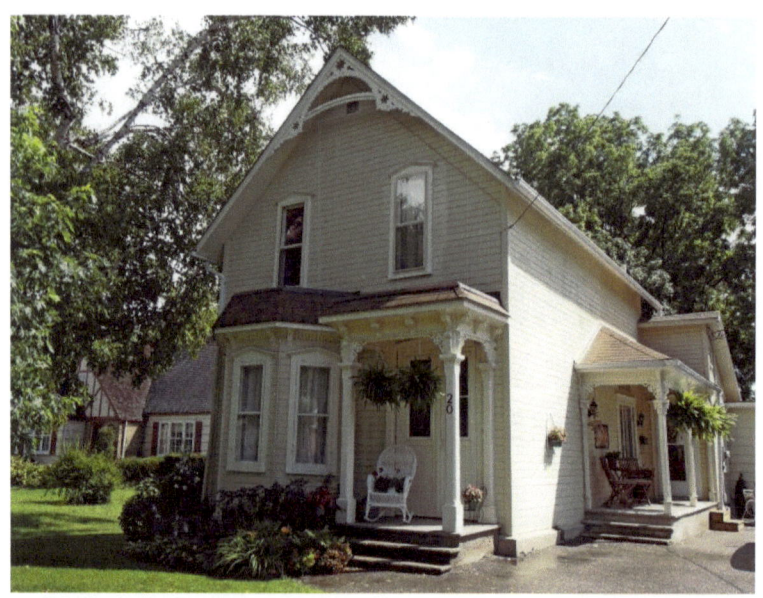

20 South Street – Gothic Revival, Vergeboard trim

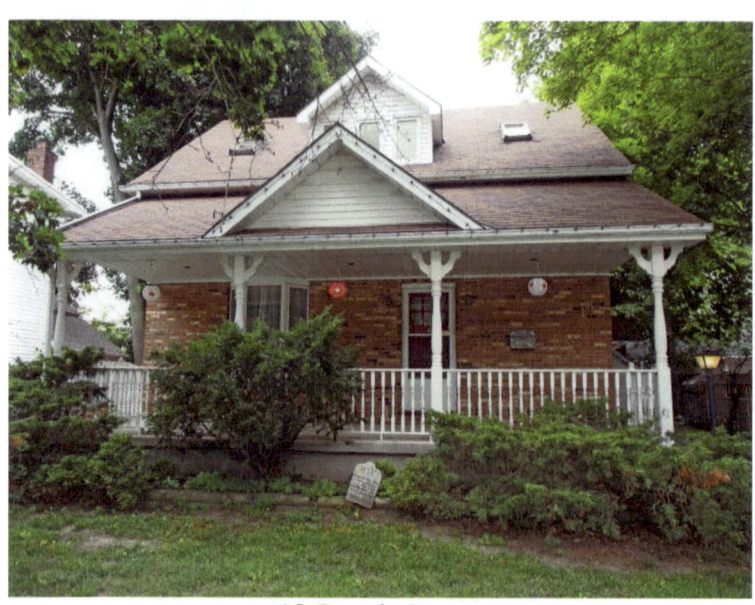

19 South Street

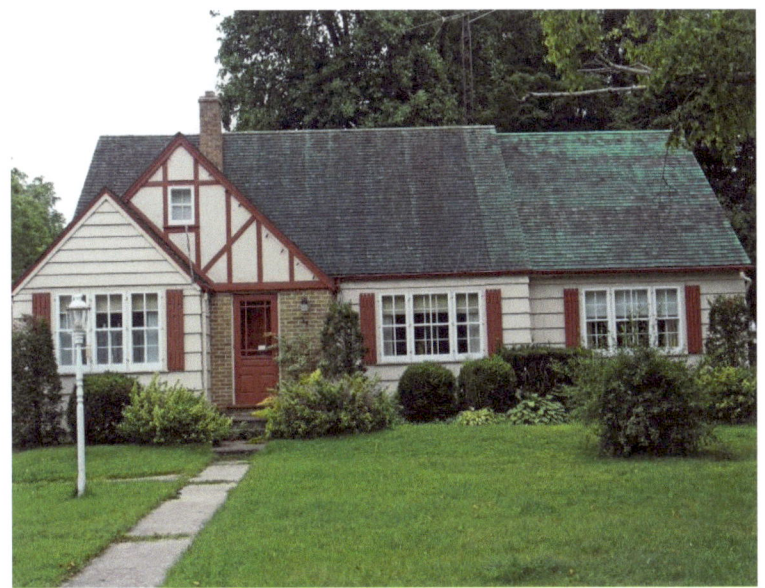

24 South Street – Tudor style

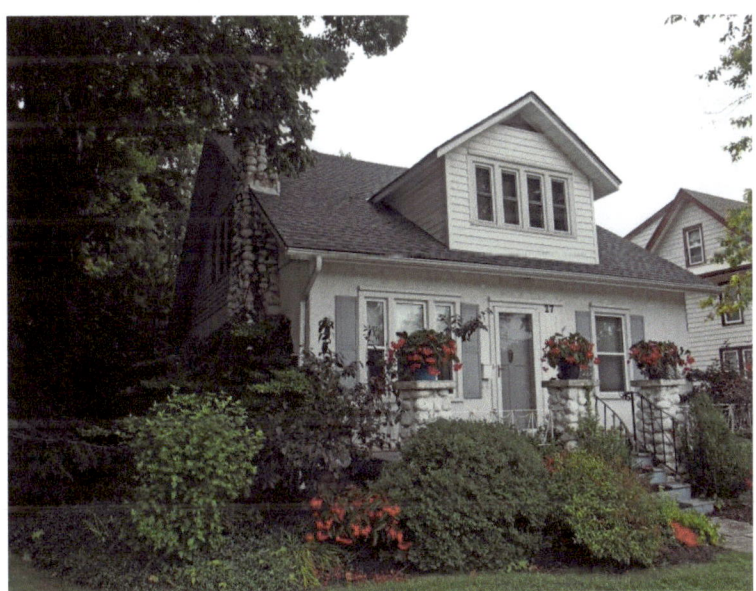

27 South Street – Gothic Revival, dormer in attic

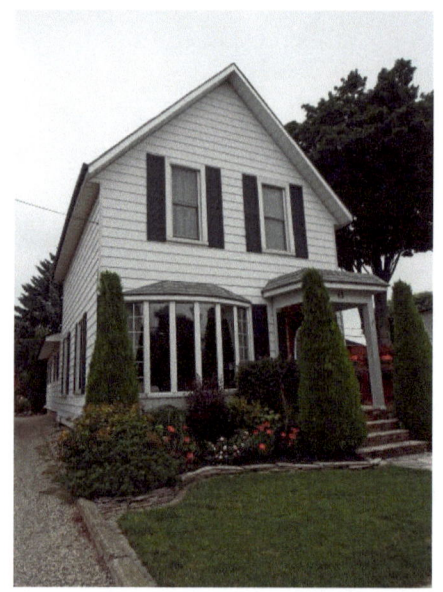

43 South Street – Gothic Revival

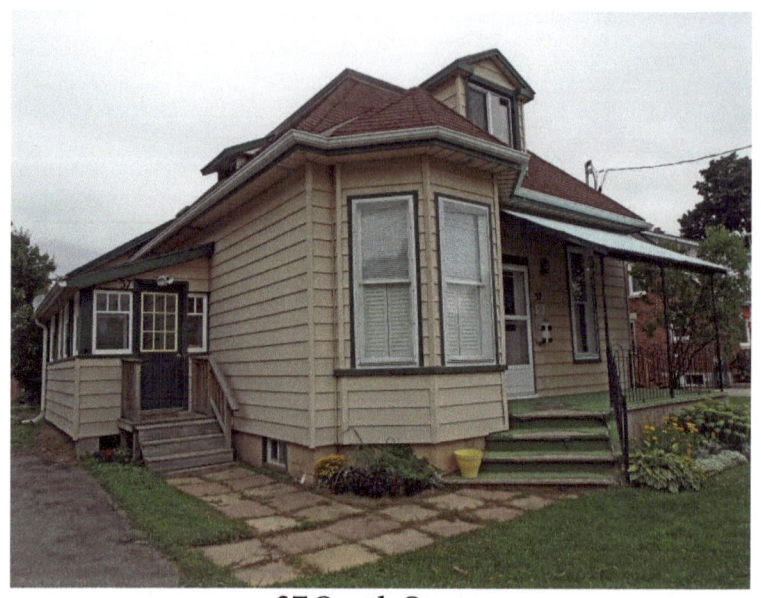

37 South Street

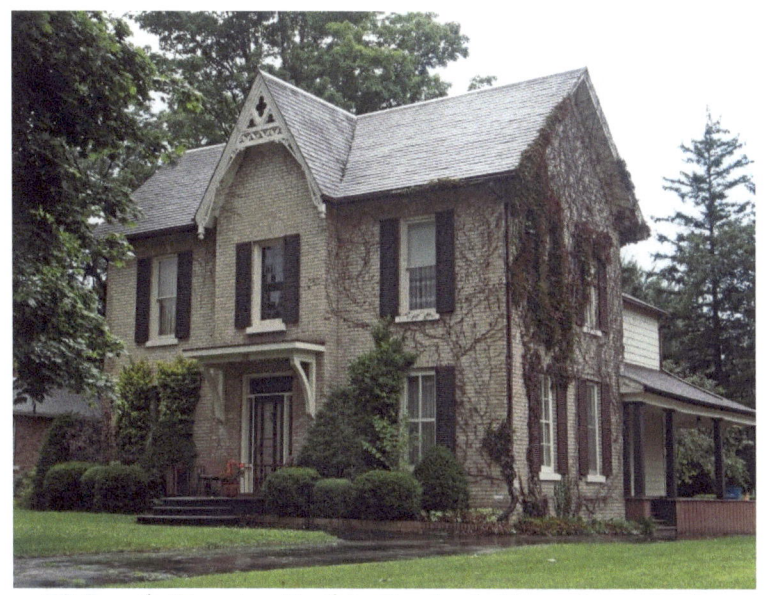

52 South Street – Gothic Revival, Vergeboard trim

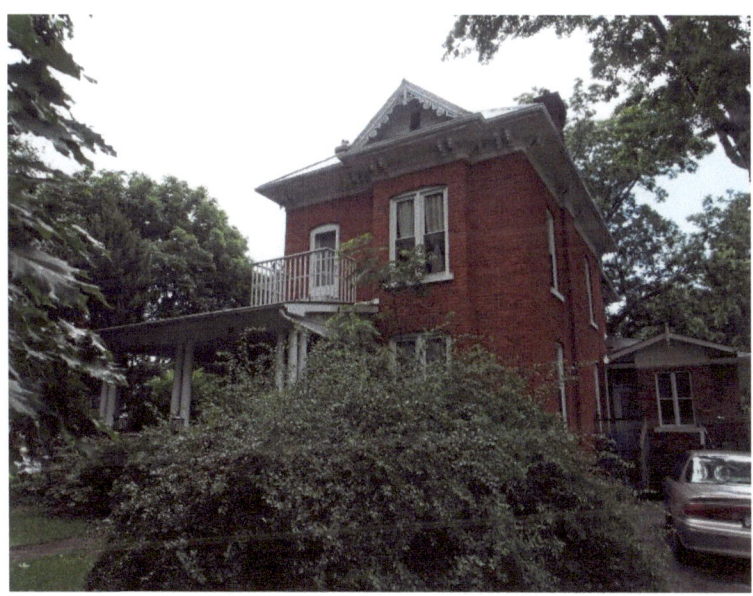

South Street – Italianate, cornice brackets, Vergeboard trim on dormer gable, second floor balcony

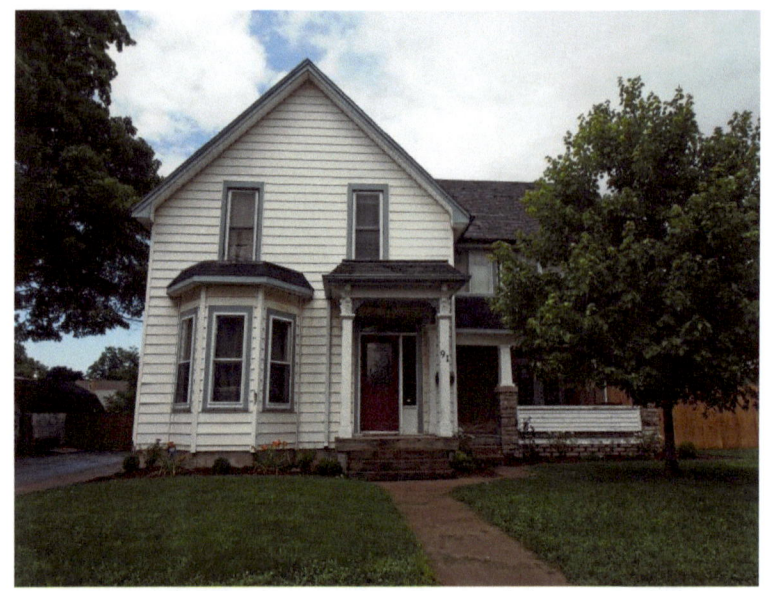

91 South Street – Gothic Revival, bay window

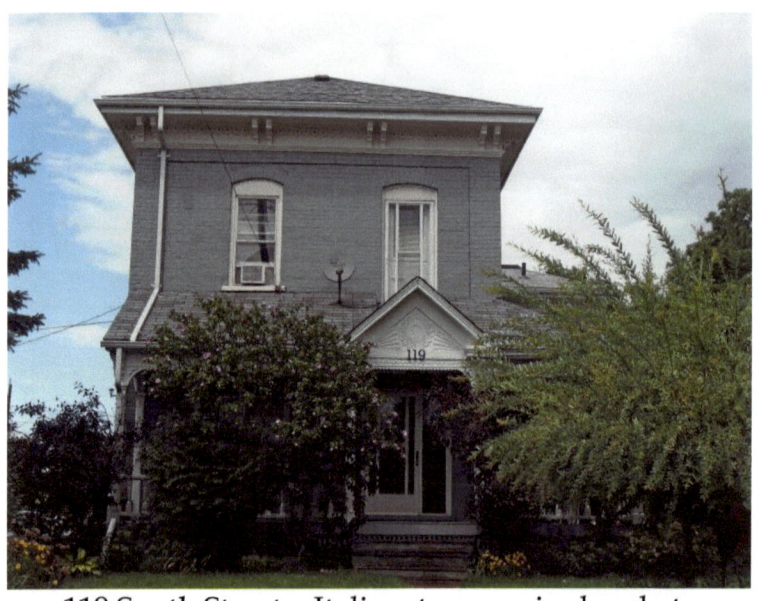

119 South Street – Italianate – cornice brackets

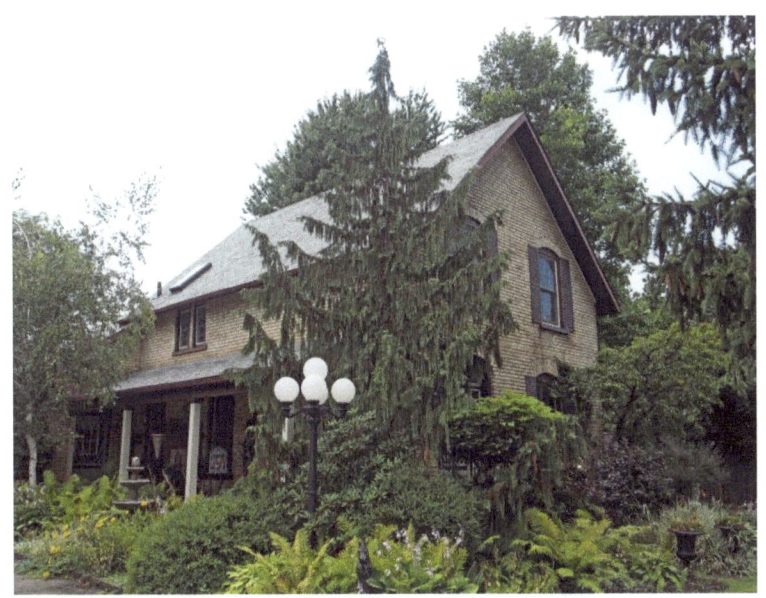

164 South Street – Gothic Revival

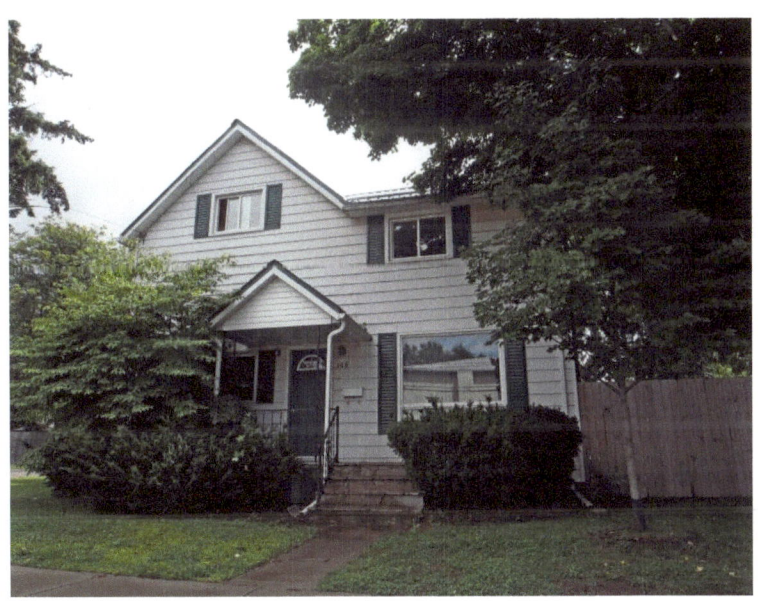

106 South Street – Gothic Revival

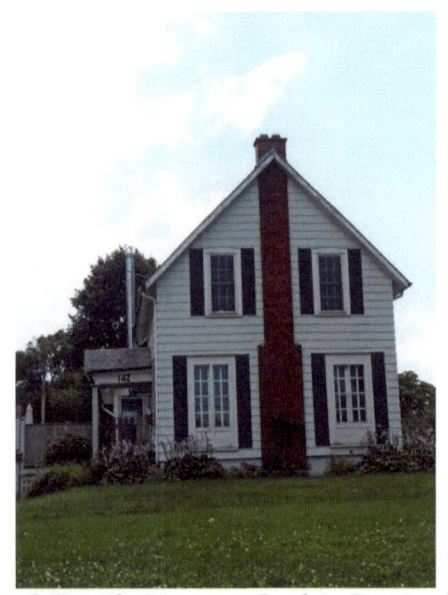

142 South Street – Gothic Revival

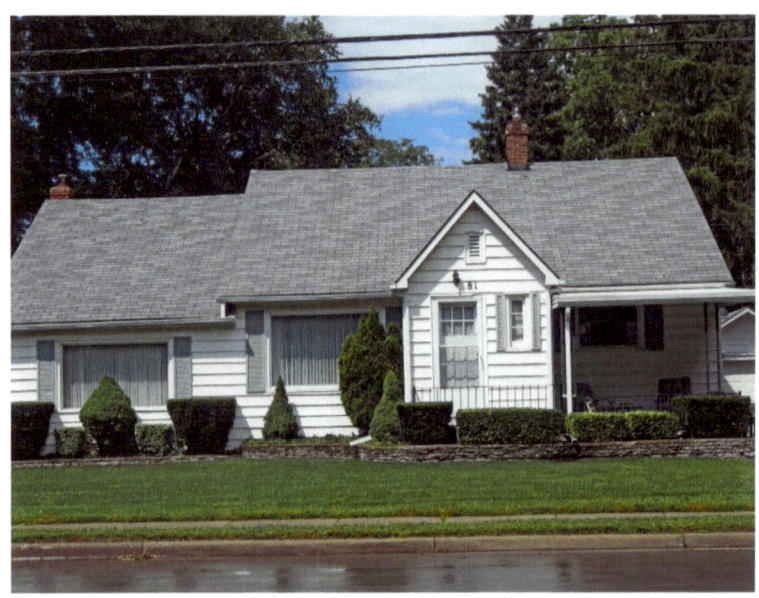

81 South Street - cottage

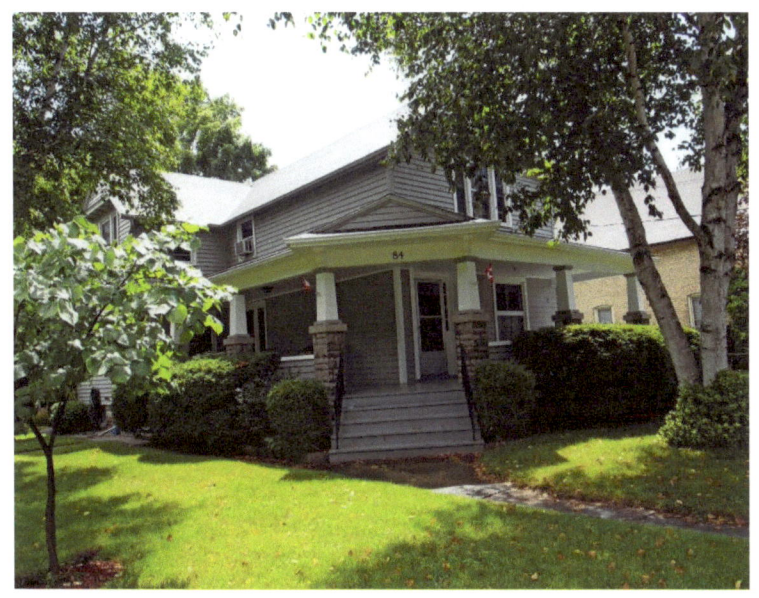

84 South Street

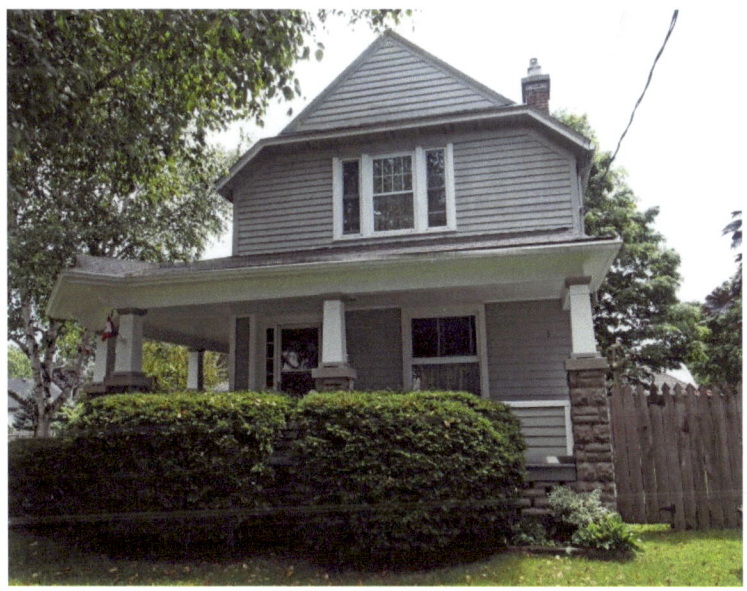

Gothic Revival

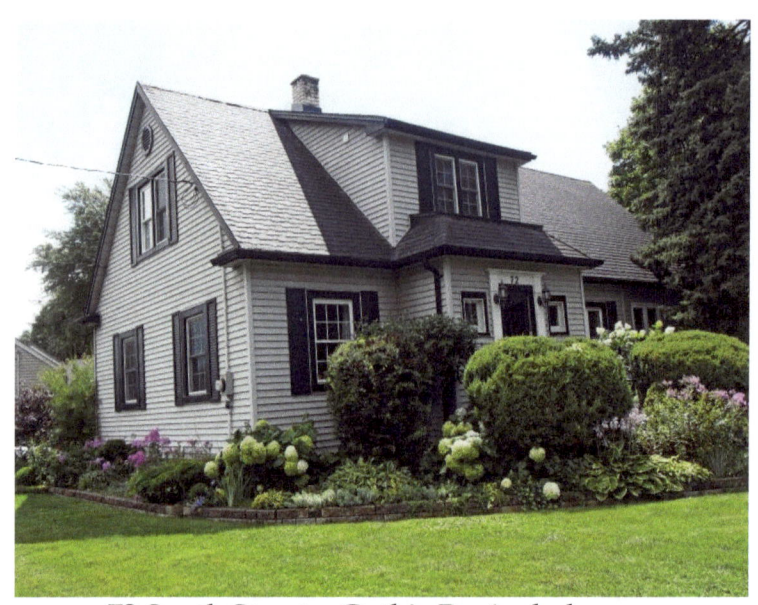

72 South Street – Gothic Revival, dormer

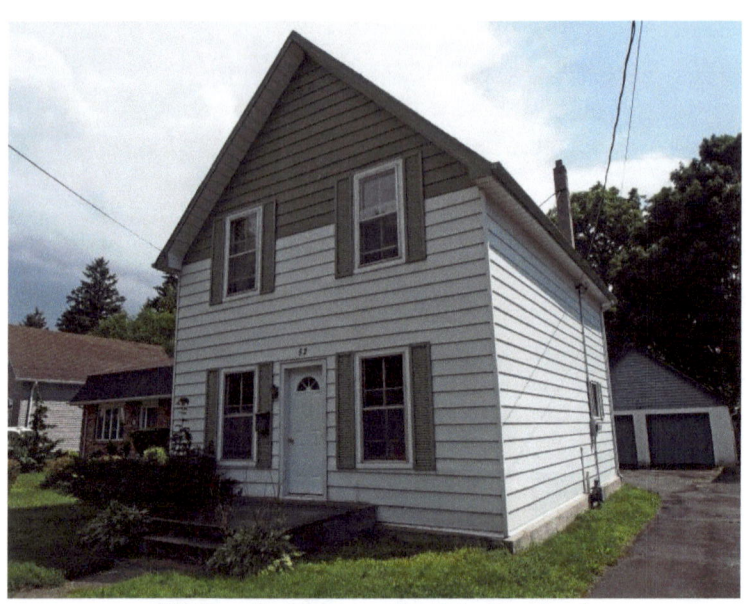

52 South Street – Gothic Revival

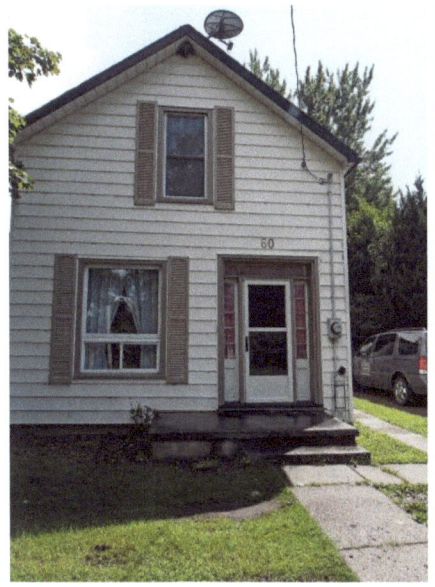

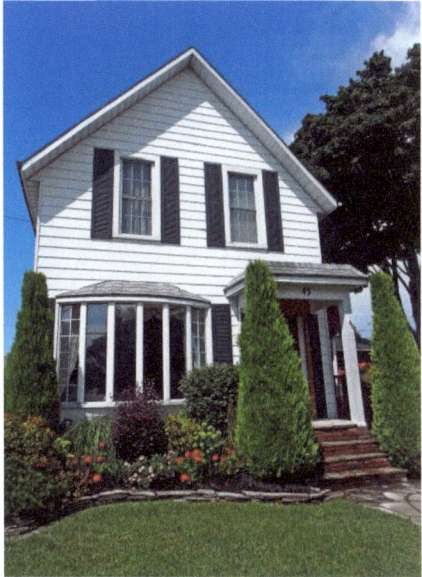

60 South Street   43 South Street

Gothic Revival

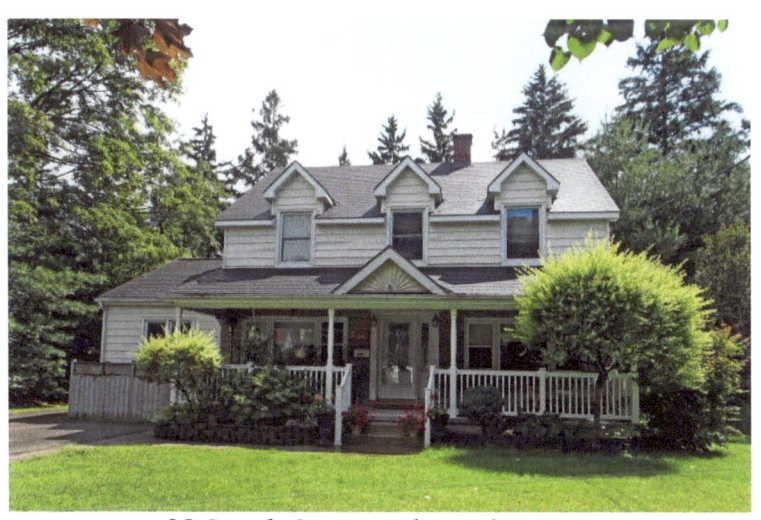

38 South Street – three dormers

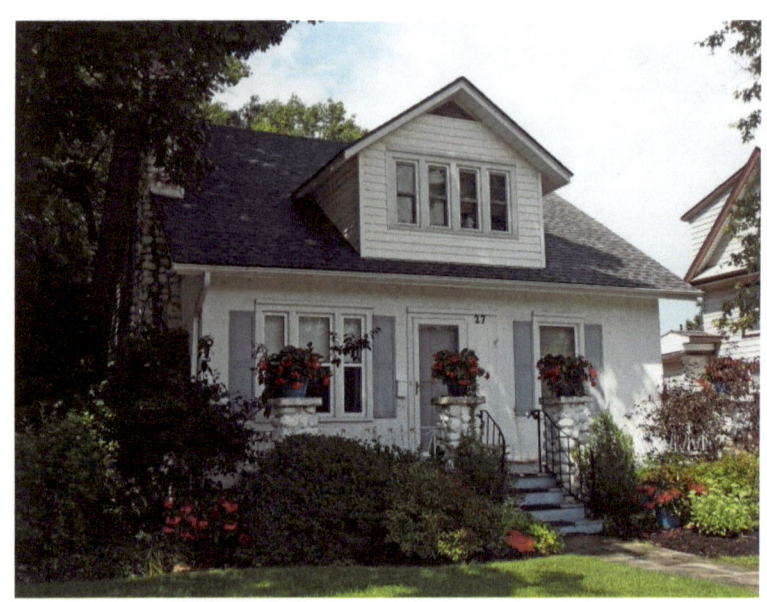

27 South Street – dormer in attic

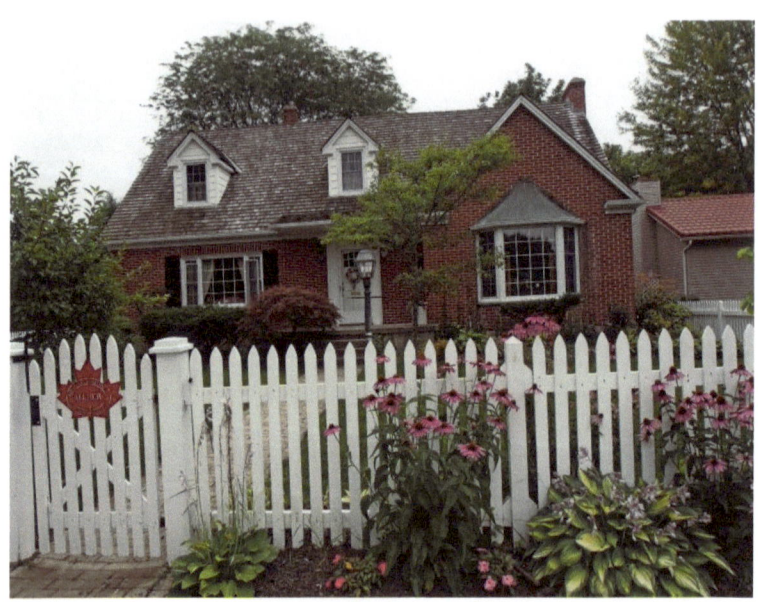

Harvey Street c. 1887

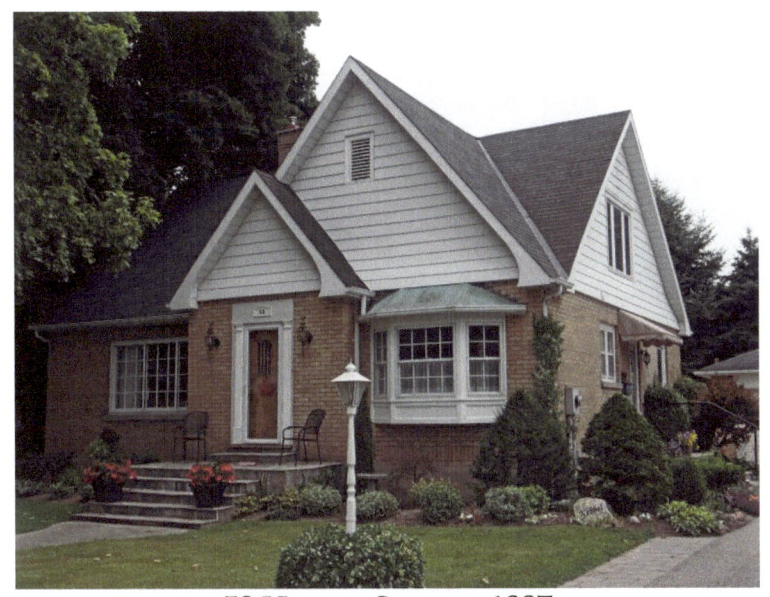

58 Harvey Street c. 1887

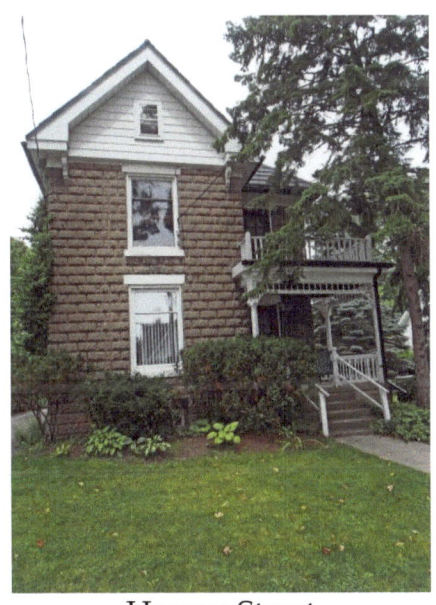

Harvey Street

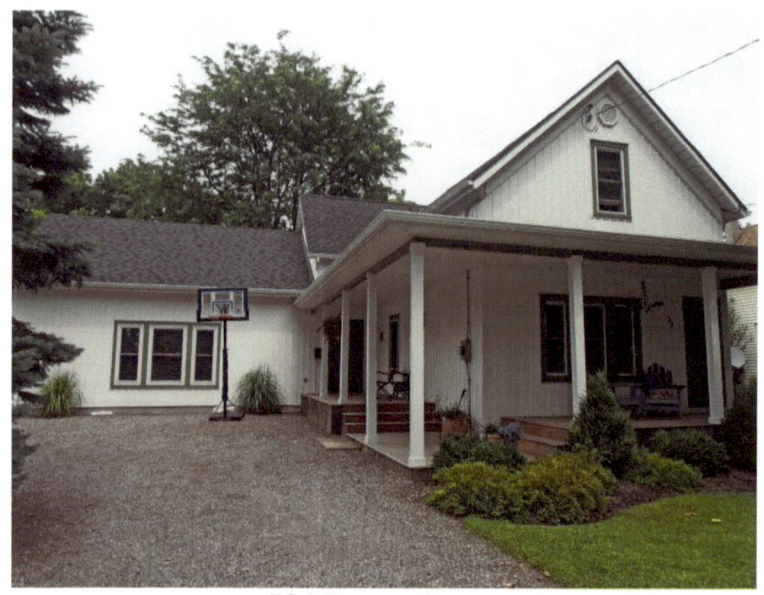

53 Harvey Street

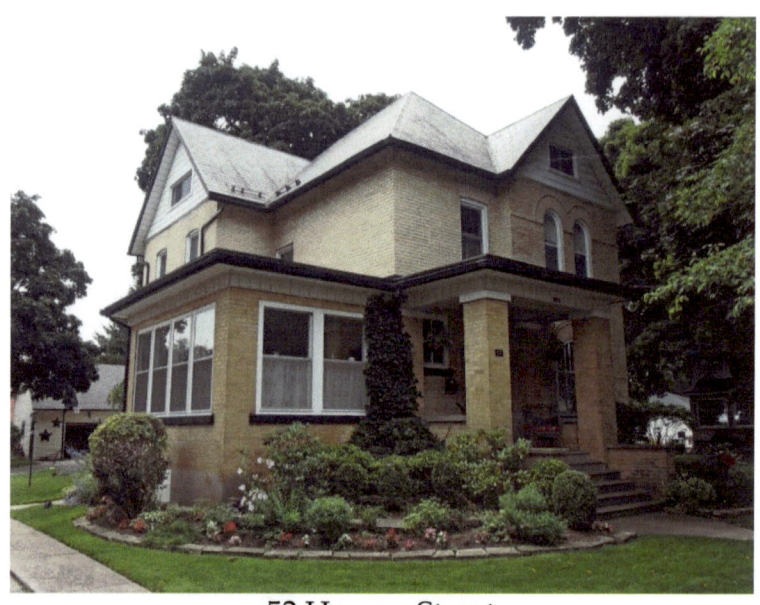

52 Harvey Street

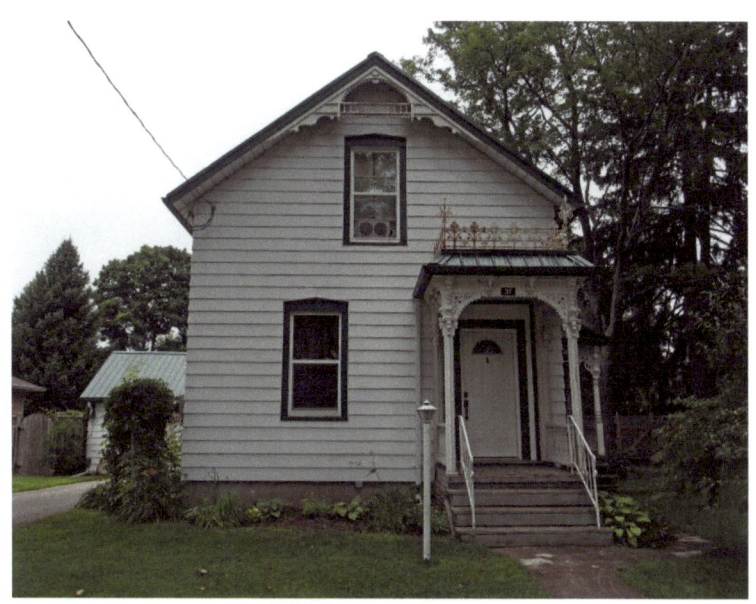

37 Harvey Street

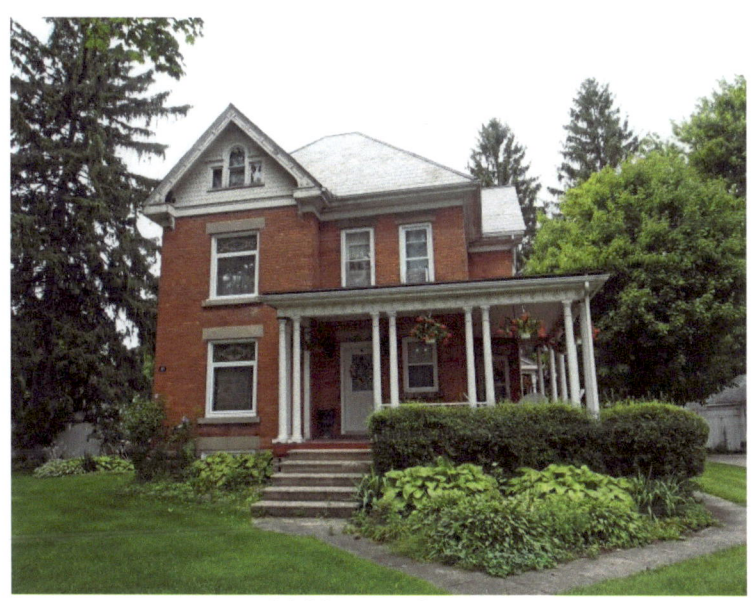

31 Harvey Street

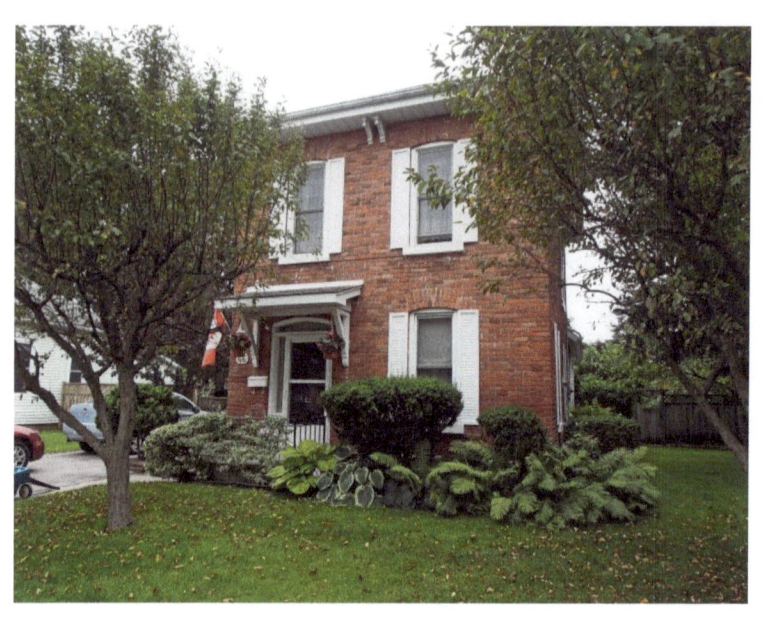

46 Harvey Street c. 1914

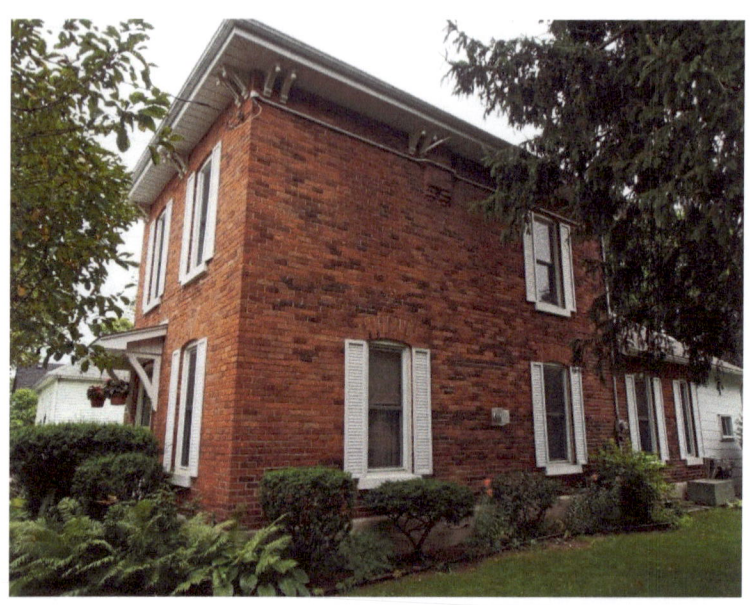

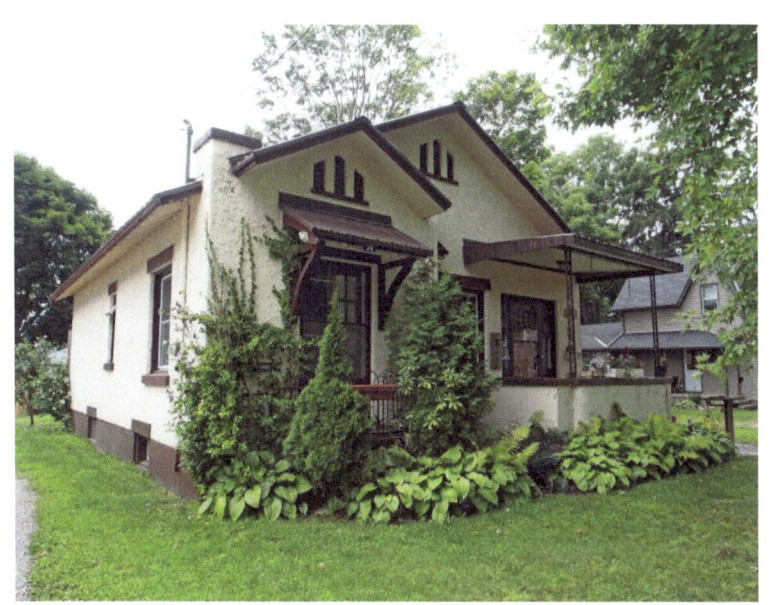

34 Harvey Street

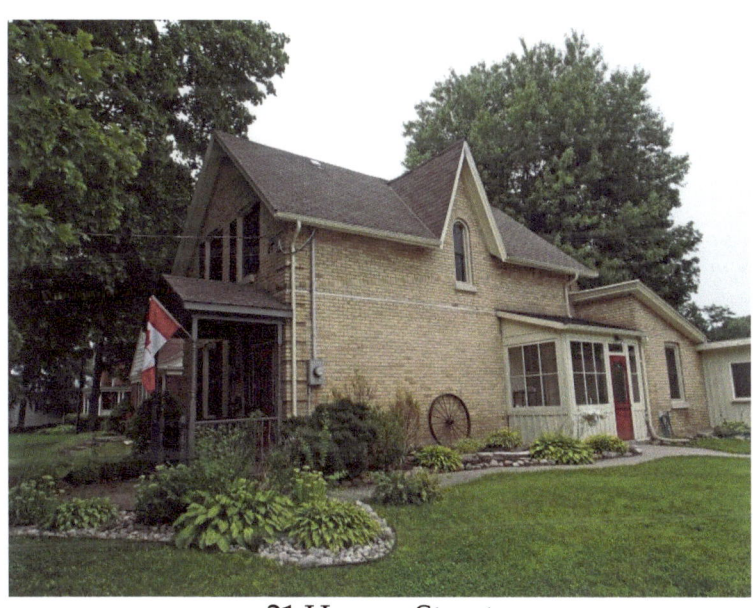

21 Harvey Street

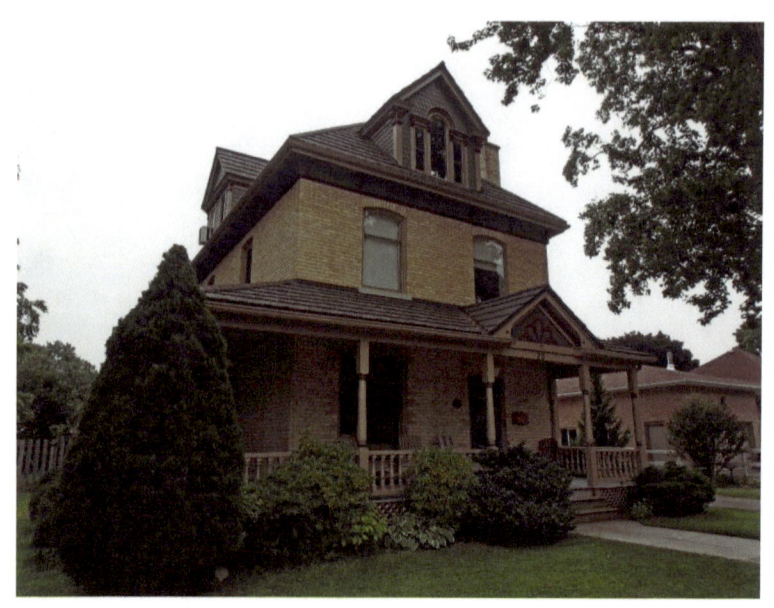

20 Harvey Street - c. 1876

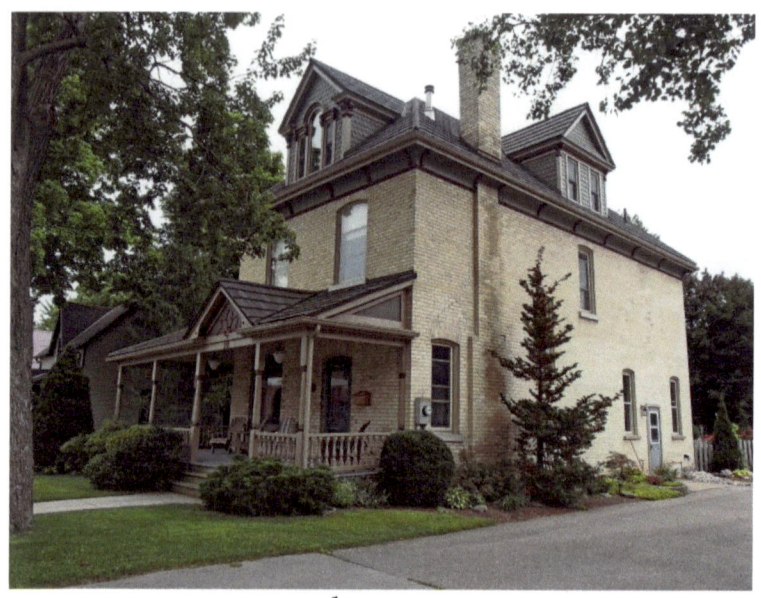

dormers

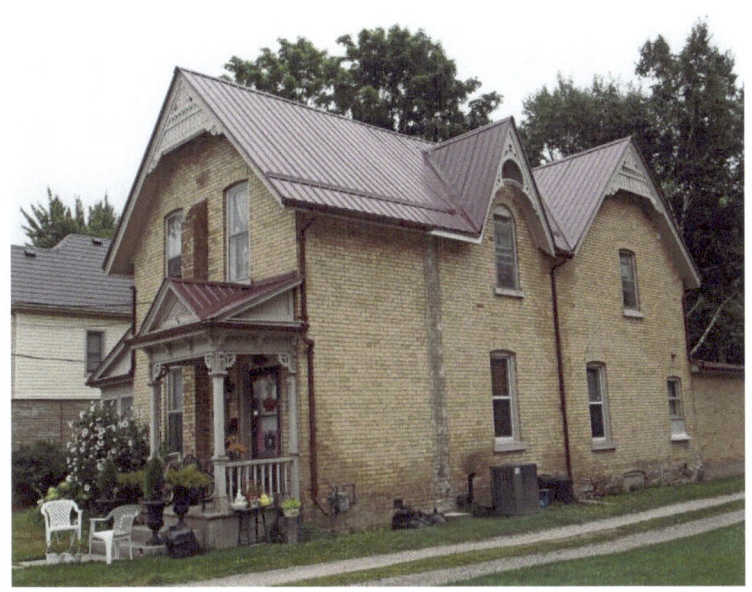

12 Harvey Street

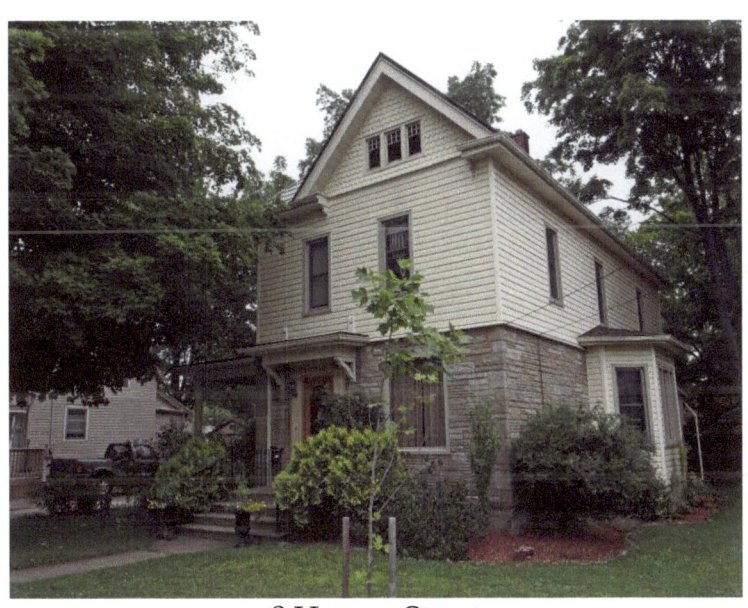

8 Harvey Street

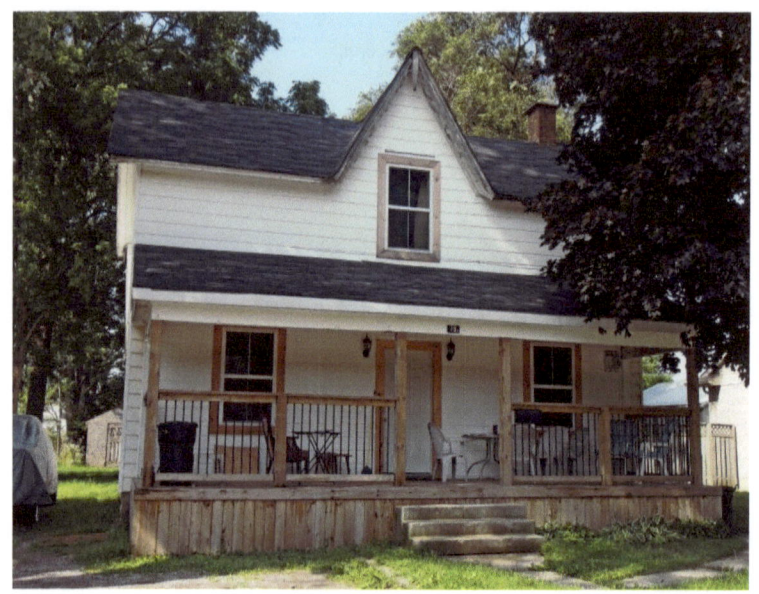

19 Forest Street

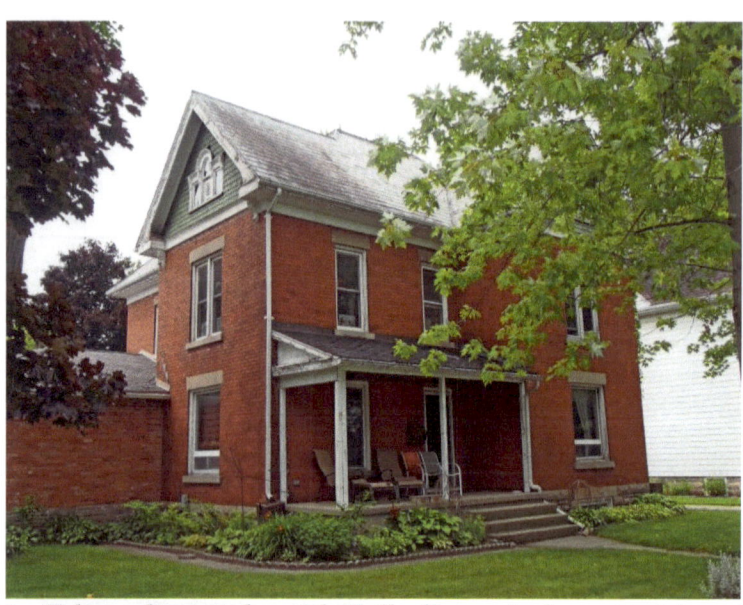

#94 – Edwardian style with Palladian window on side gable

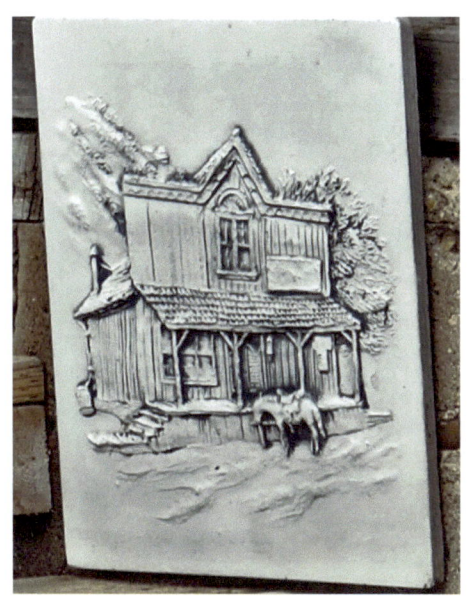

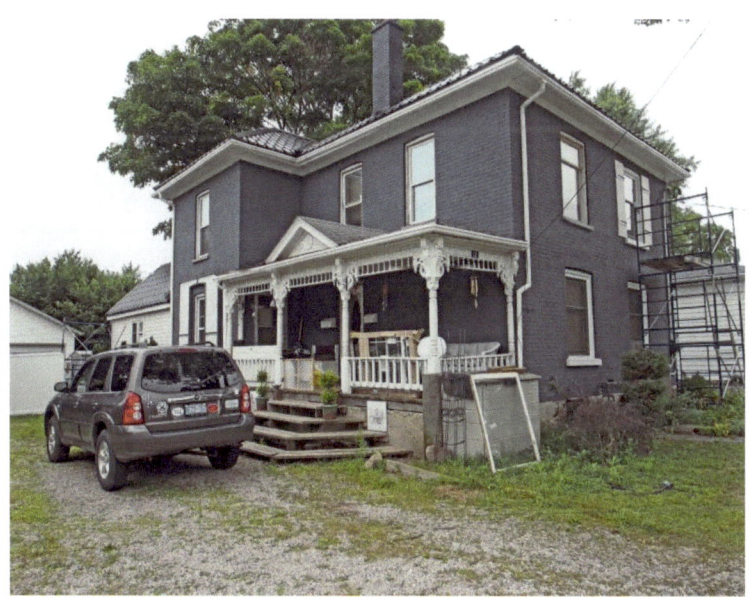

12 Clarence Street

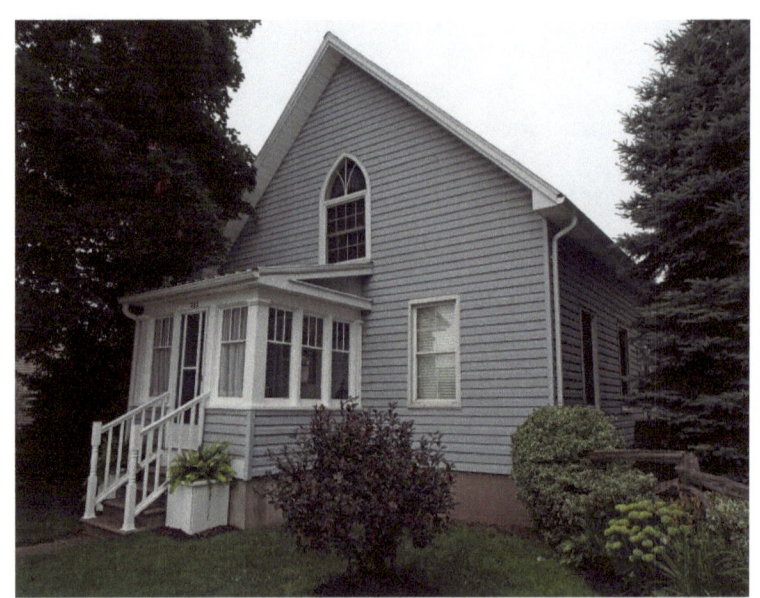

242 John Street South – Gothic Revival

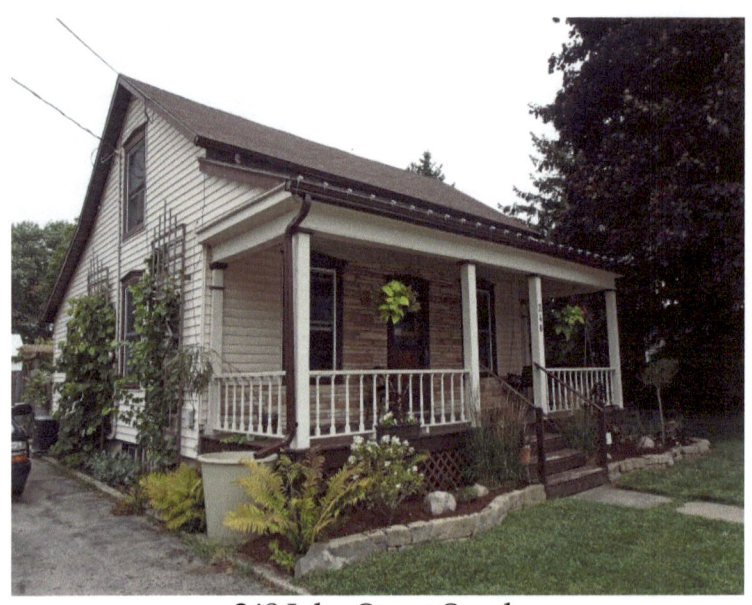

248 John Street South

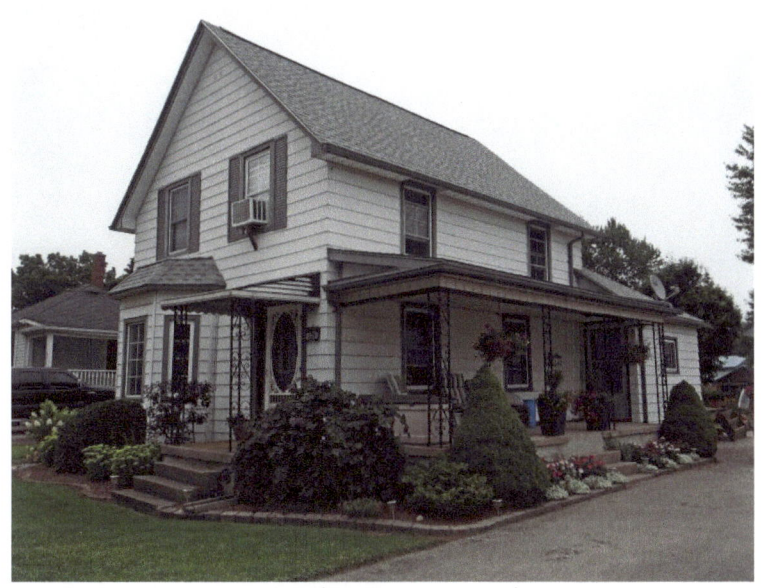

239 John Street South

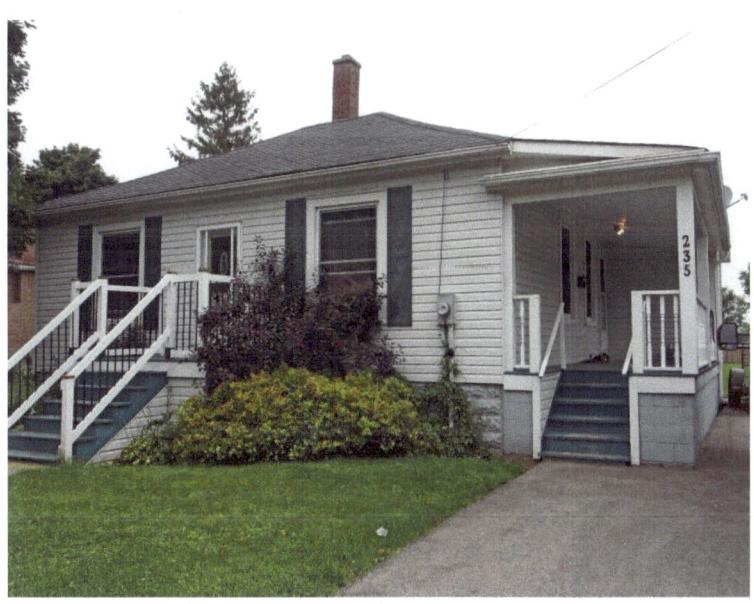

235 John Street South – Regency Cottage

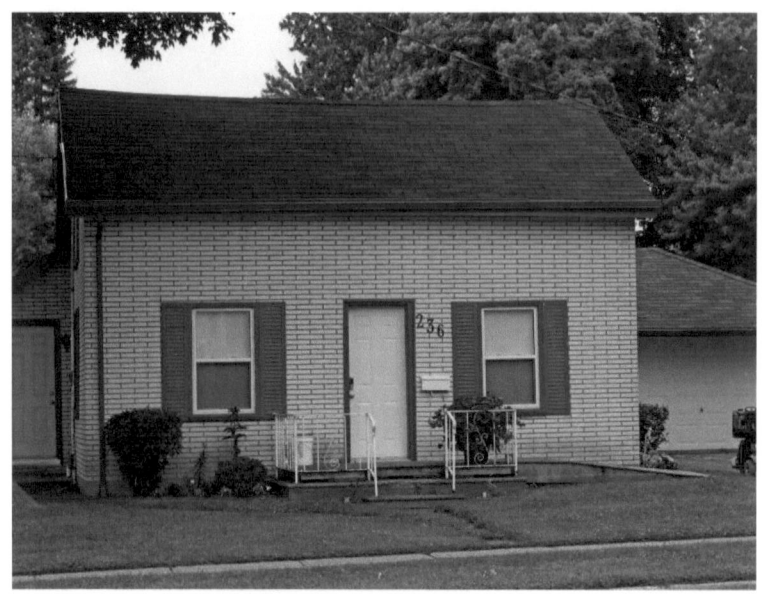

236 John Street South

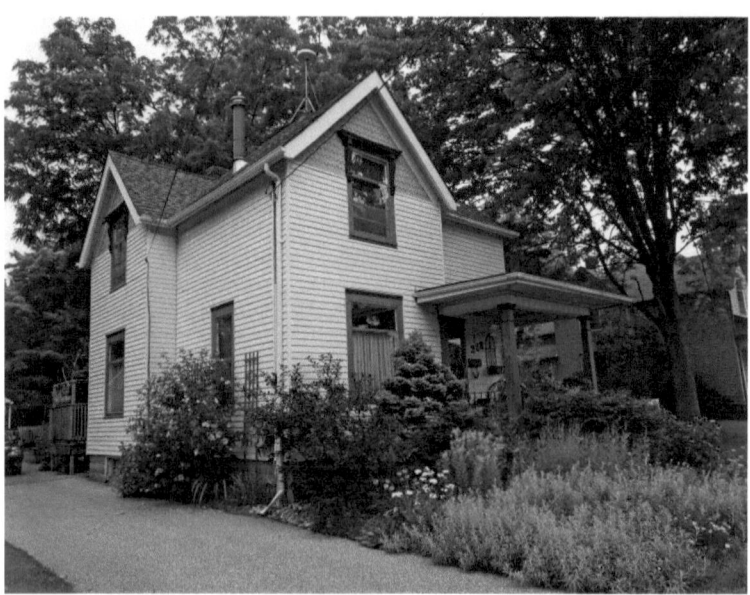

228 John Street South – Gothic Revival

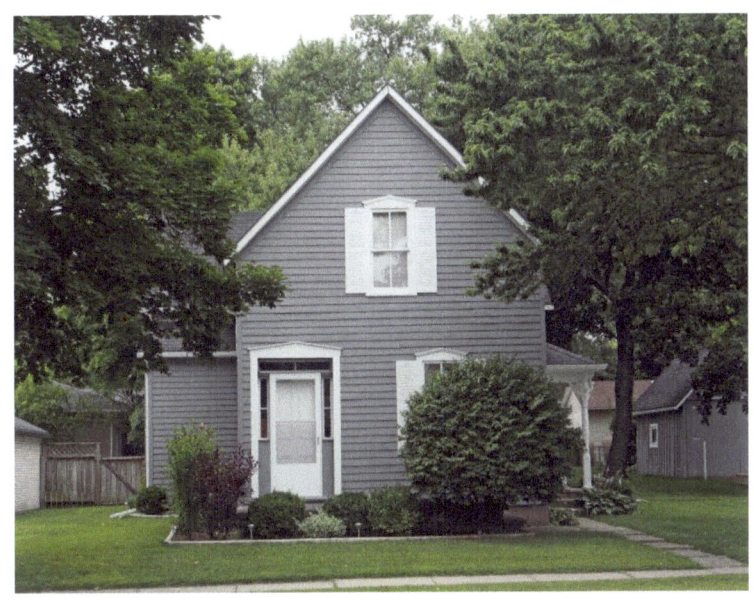

232 John Street South – Gothic Revival

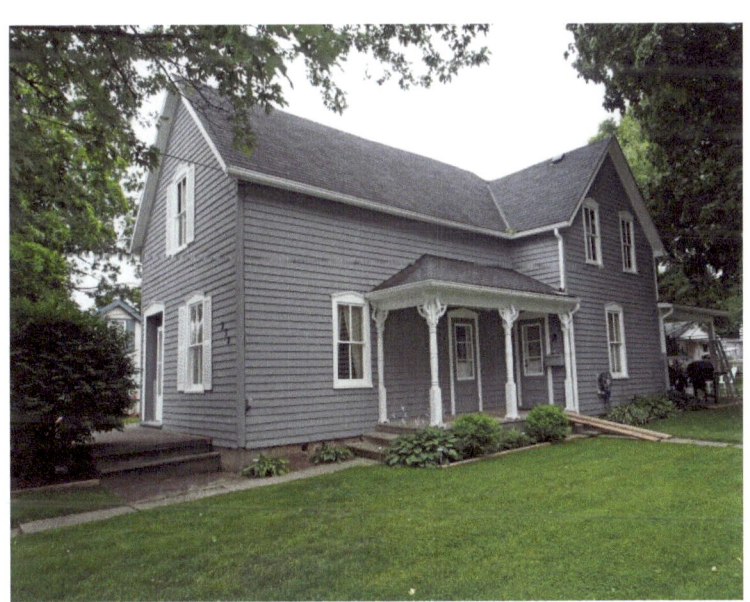

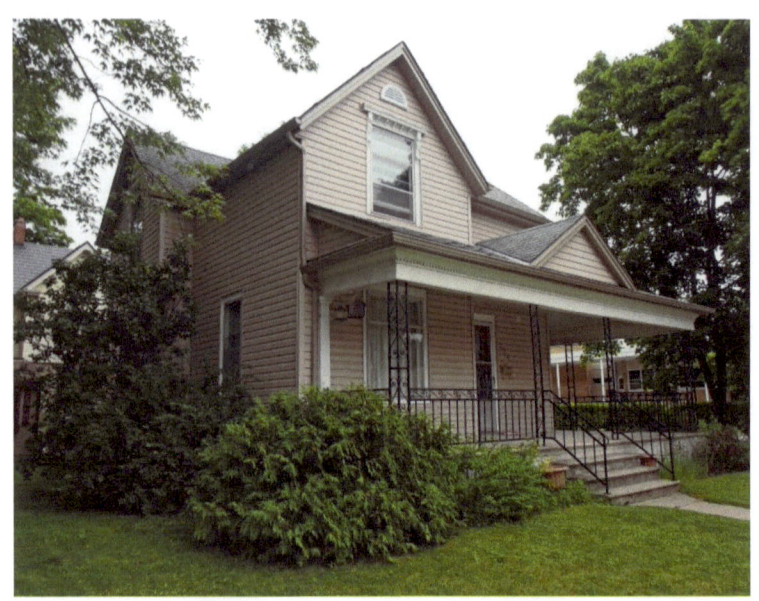

224 John Street South - Gothic

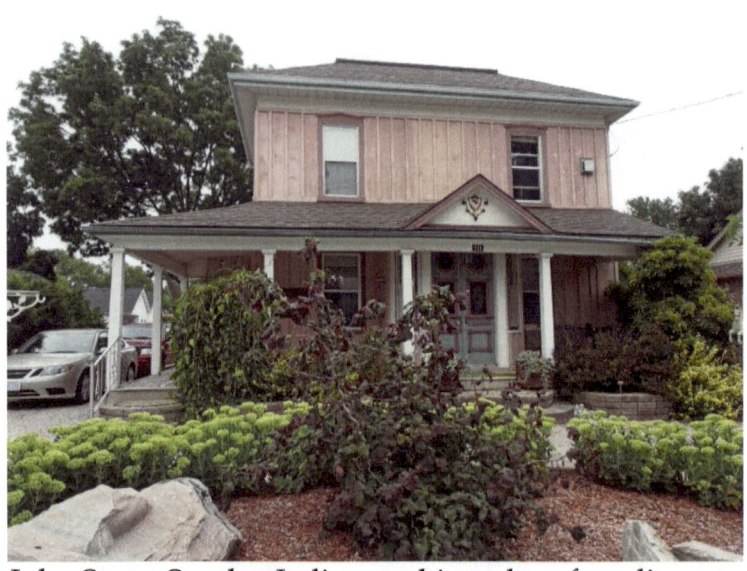

221 John Street South – Italianate, hipped roof, pediment with decorative tympanum

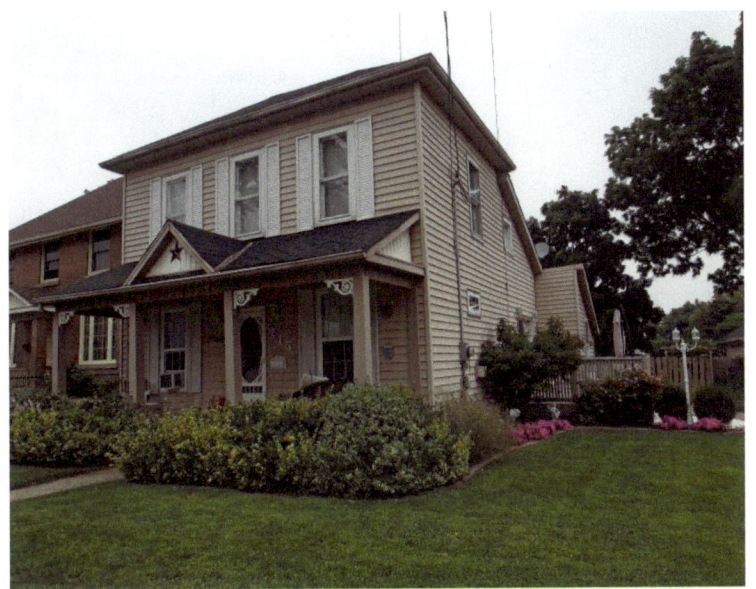

215 John Street South – Italianate, hipped roof

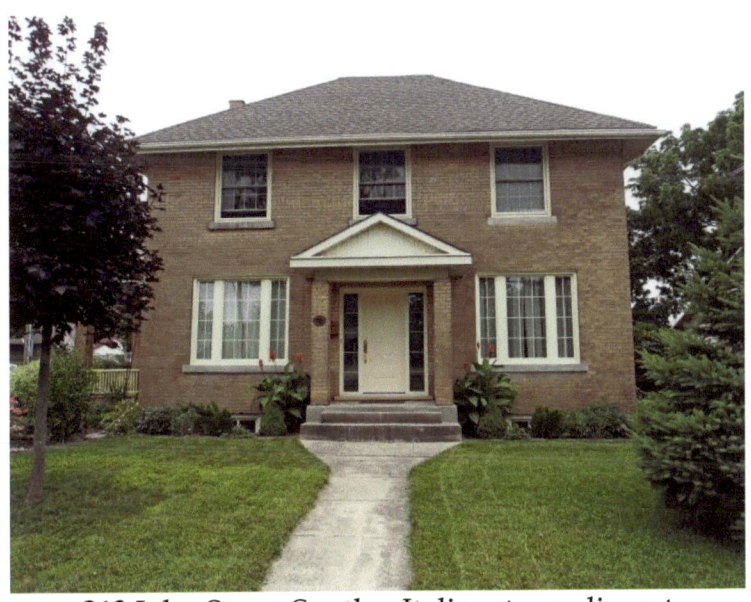

213 John Street South – Italianate, pediment

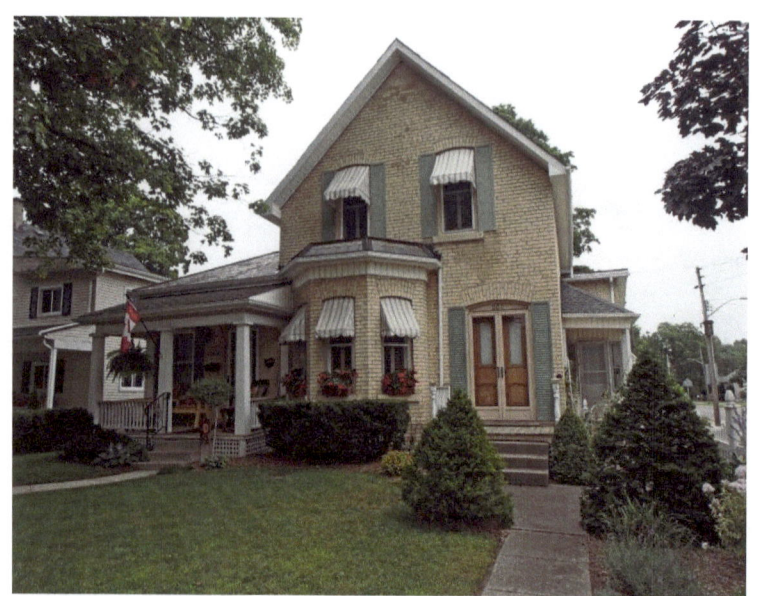

207 John Street South – Gothic Revival, bay window

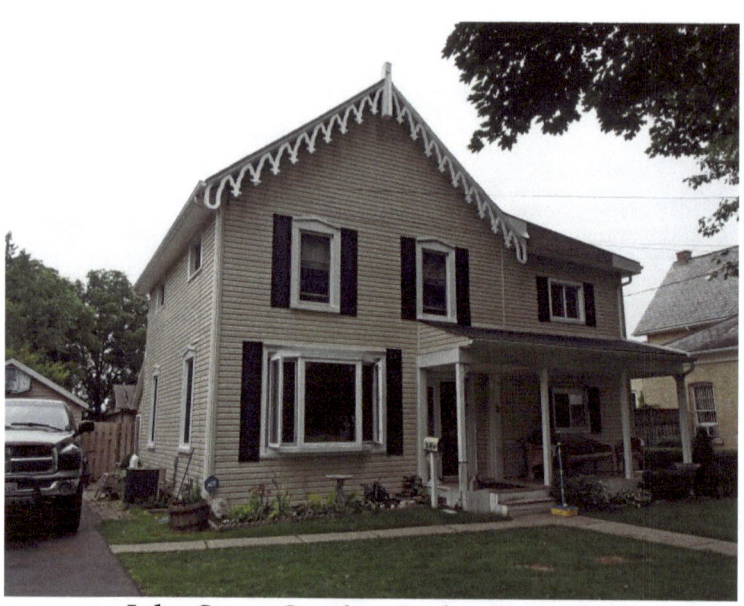

John Street South – Gothic Revival –
Vergeboard trim and finial on gable

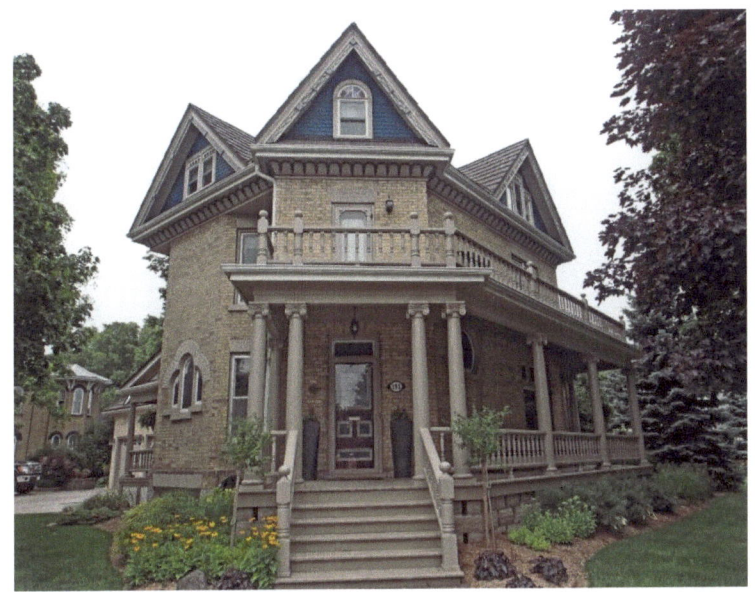

193 John Street South – Queen Anne style – c. 1899
Ionic columns with scroll-like capitals

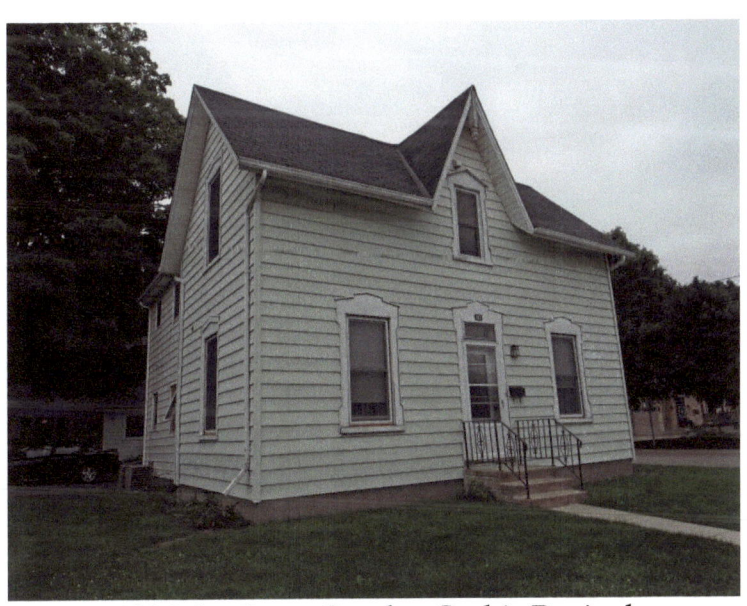

183 John Street South – Gothic Revival

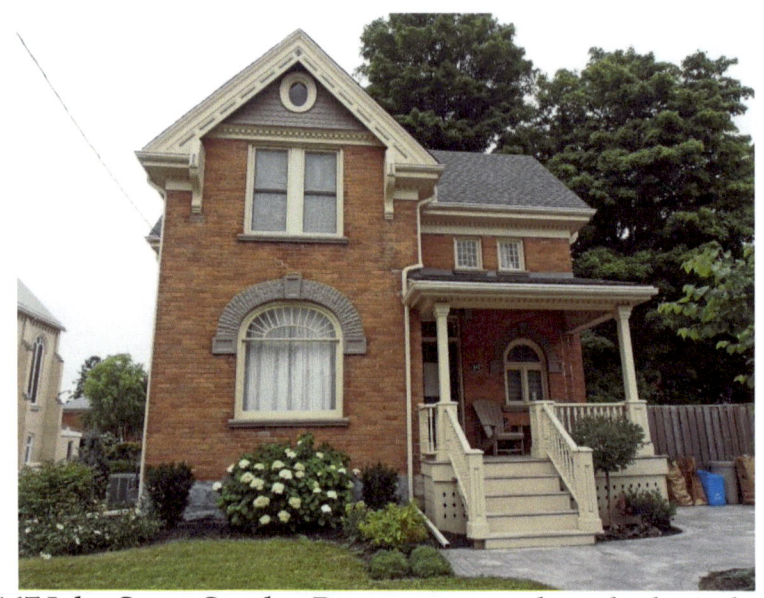

167 John Street South – Romanesque style arched window voussoirs

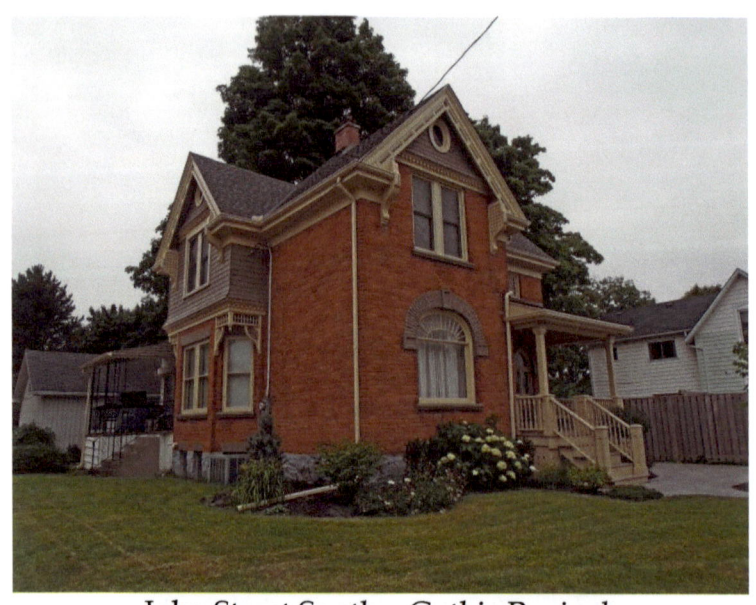

John Street South – Gothic Revival,
Romanesque like window voussoirs

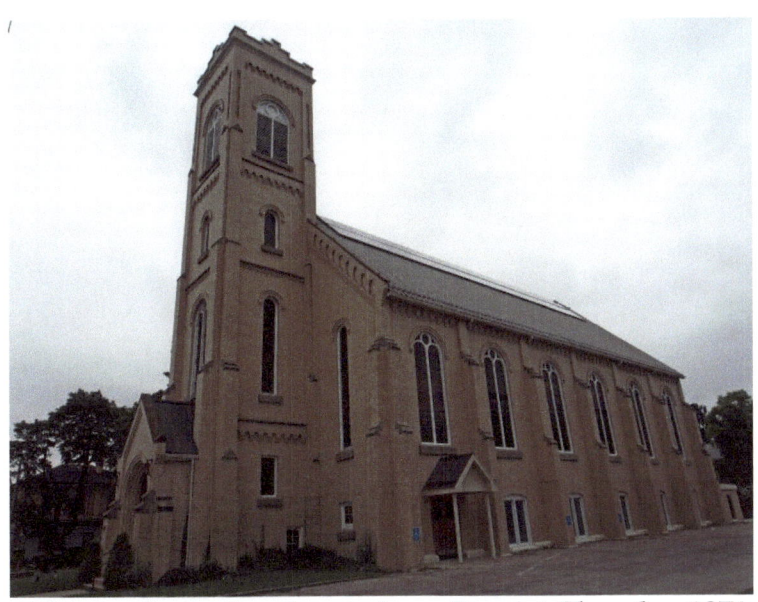

153 John Street South – Aylmer Baptist Church – 1871
Buttresses, lancet windows, bell tower

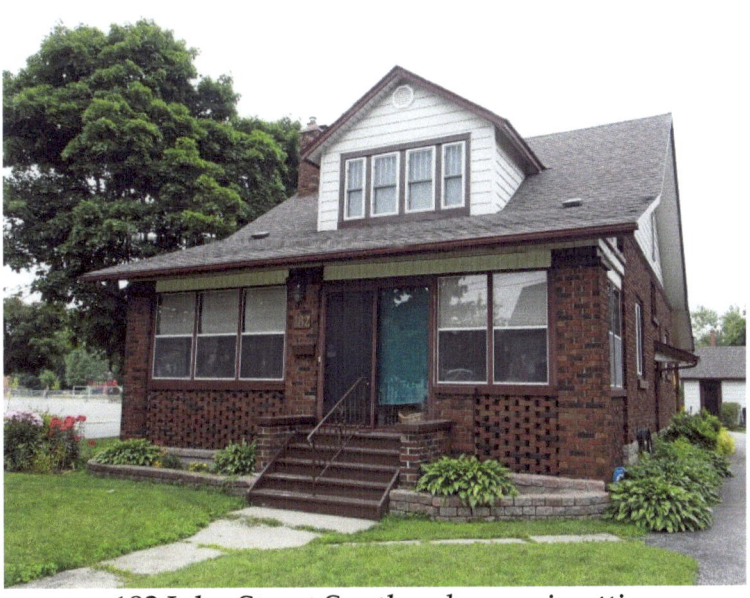

182 John Street South – dormer in attic

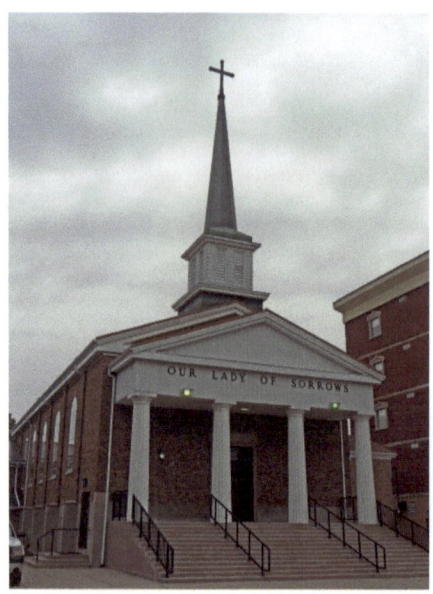

John Street South - Our Lady of Sorrows

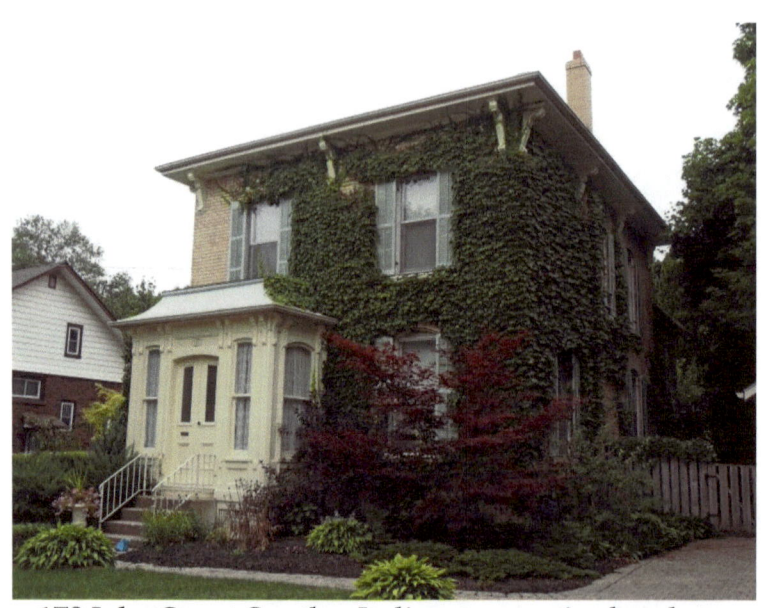

170 John Street South – Italianate, cornice brackets, hipped roof

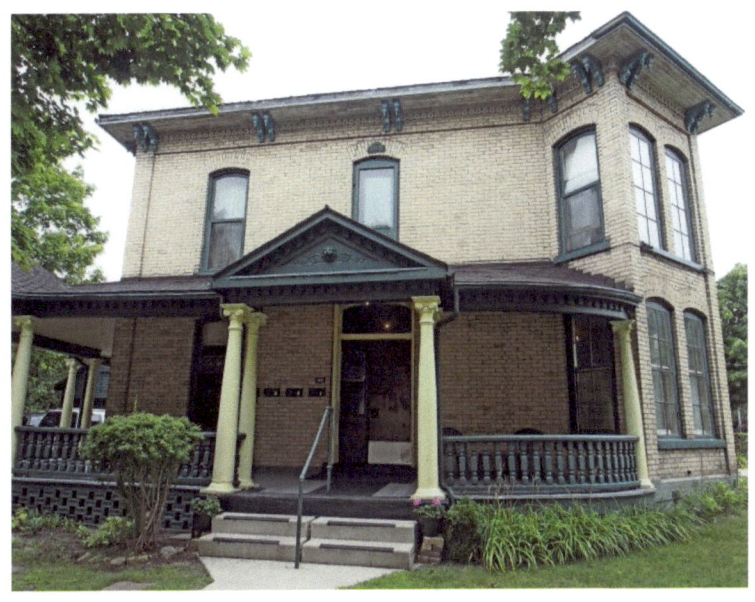

148 John Street South – Italianate, pediment, cornice brackets

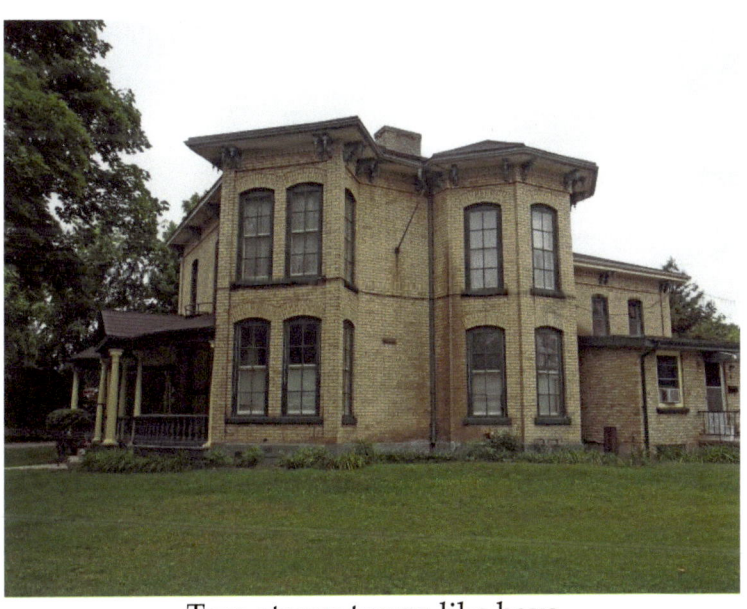

Two-storey tower-like bays

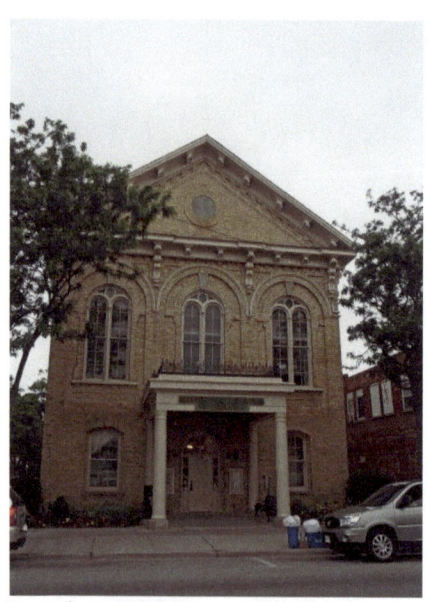

38 John Street South – Old Town Hall Theatre and Library – built in 1874 in Italianate style, Romanesque window arches (arcaded brickwork), Florentine windows, iron cresting above entranceway, cornice brackets, boldly-modelled cornice

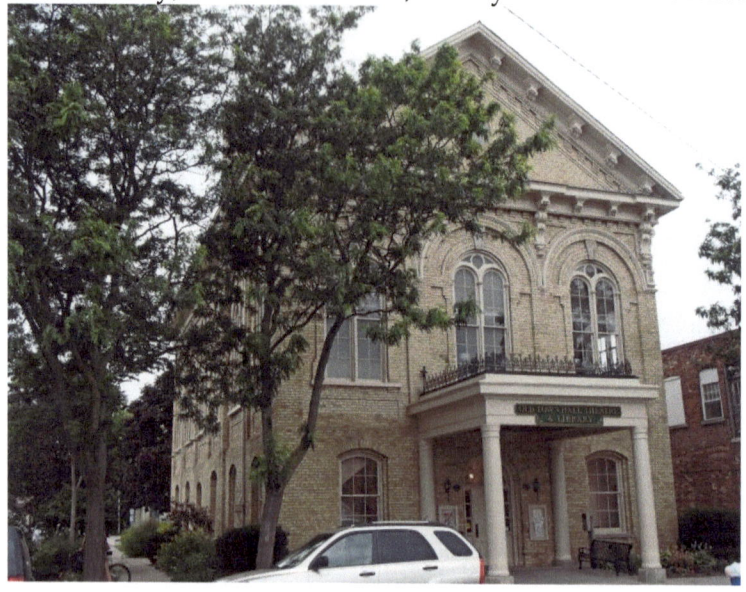

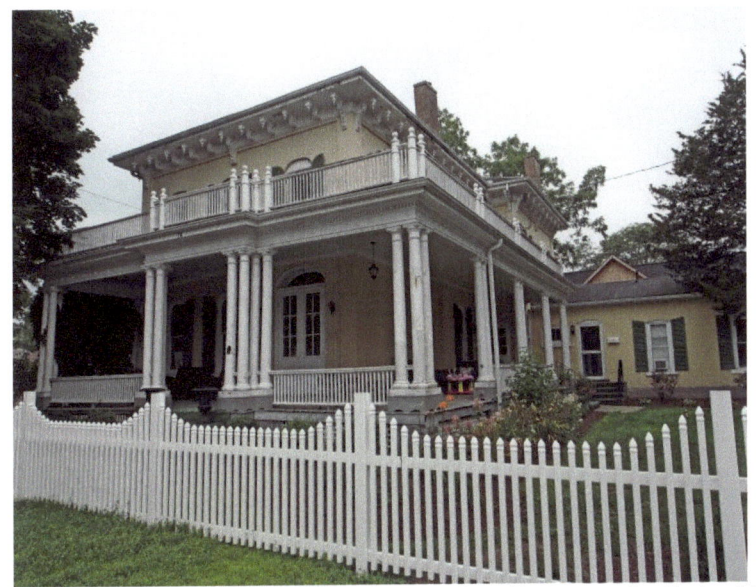

76 King Street – Italianate, Bingham/Dell House built in 1868
25 pillars adorn the wraparound verandah, cornice brackets

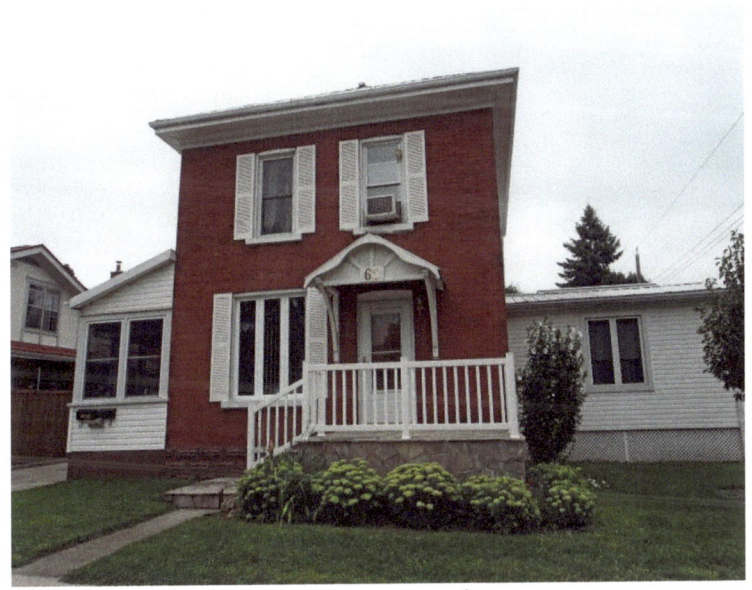

65 King Street – Italianate

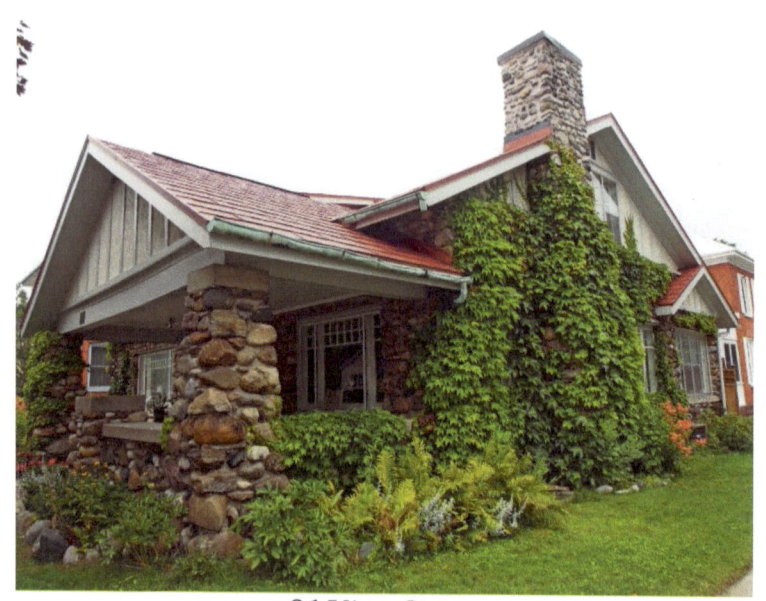

86 King Street

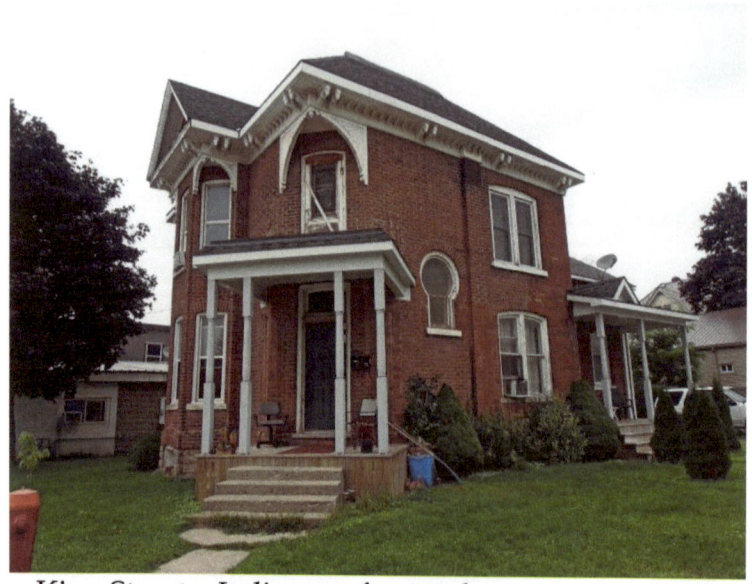

King Street – Italianate, fretwork, cornice brackets, keyhole window

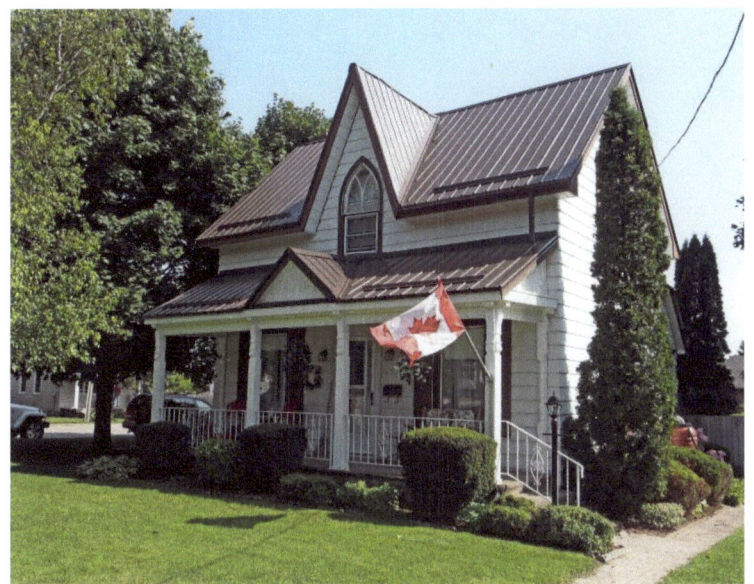

14 Maple Street – Gothic Revival, pediment

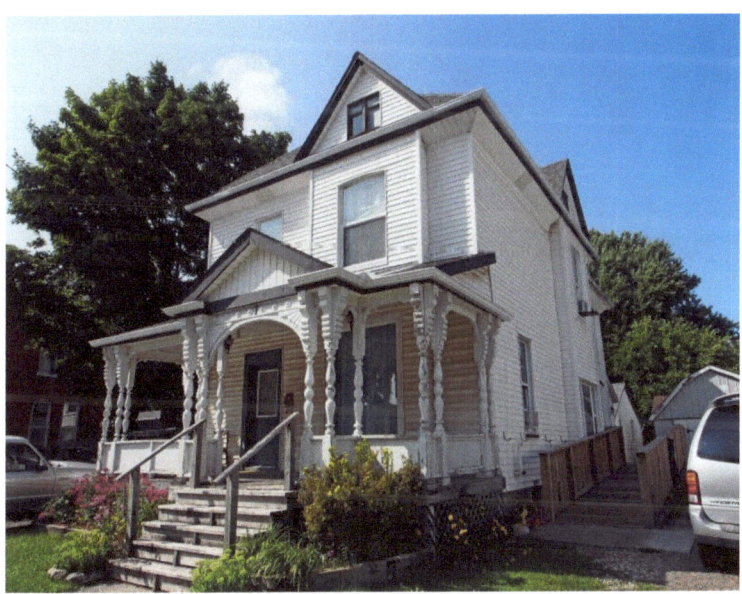

7 Maple Street, pediment, decorative lathe-turned pillars

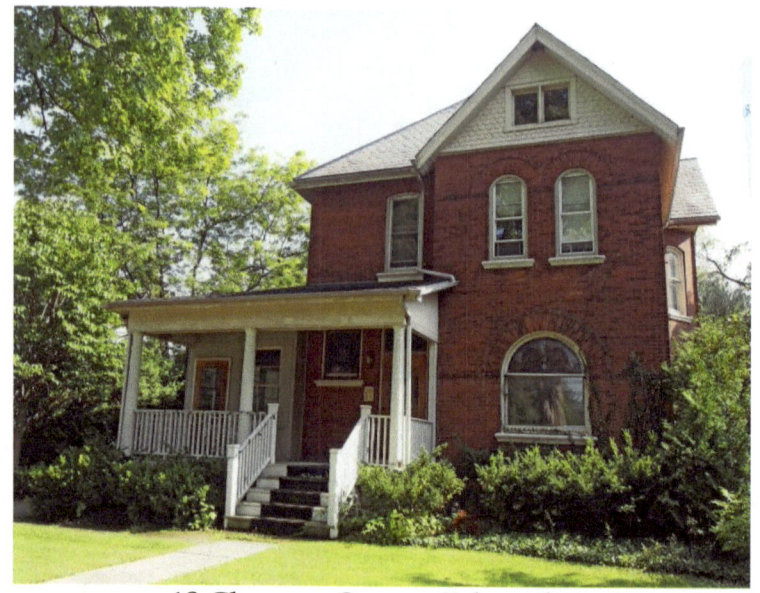

18 Chestnut Street - Edwardian

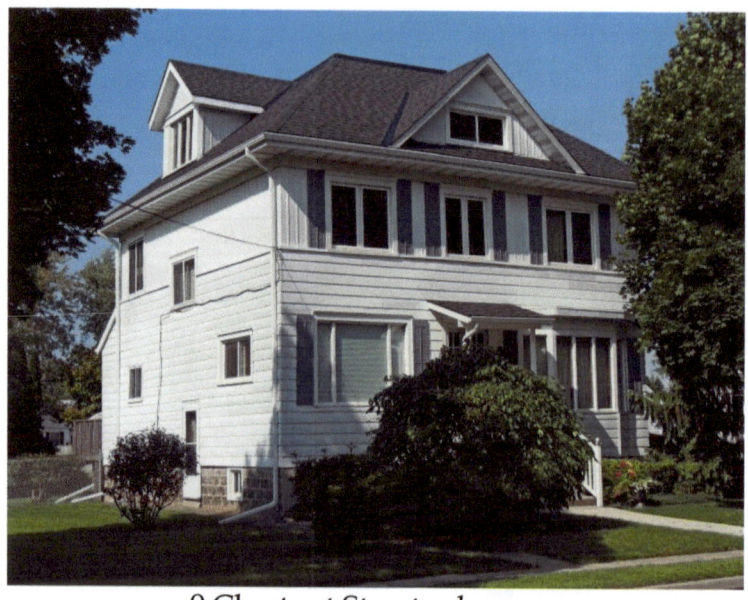

9 Chestnut Street - dormers

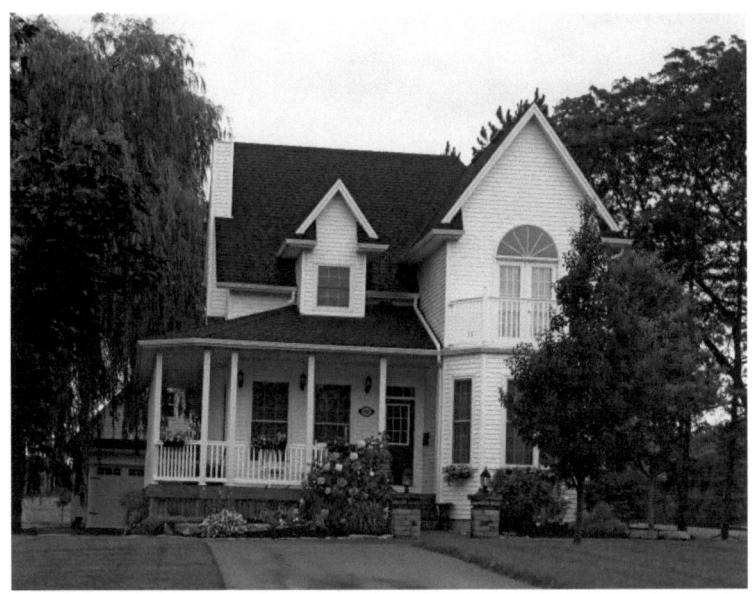

400 Oak Street

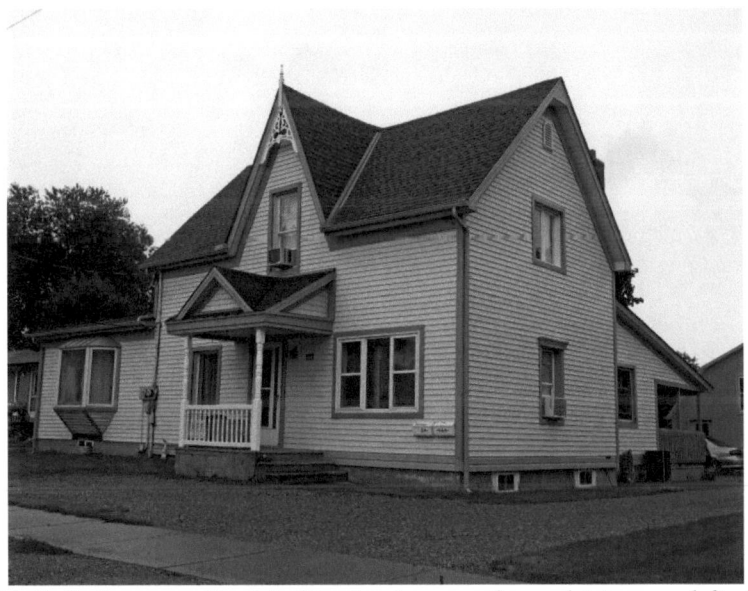

404 Oak Street – Gothic Revival, vergeboard trim and finial

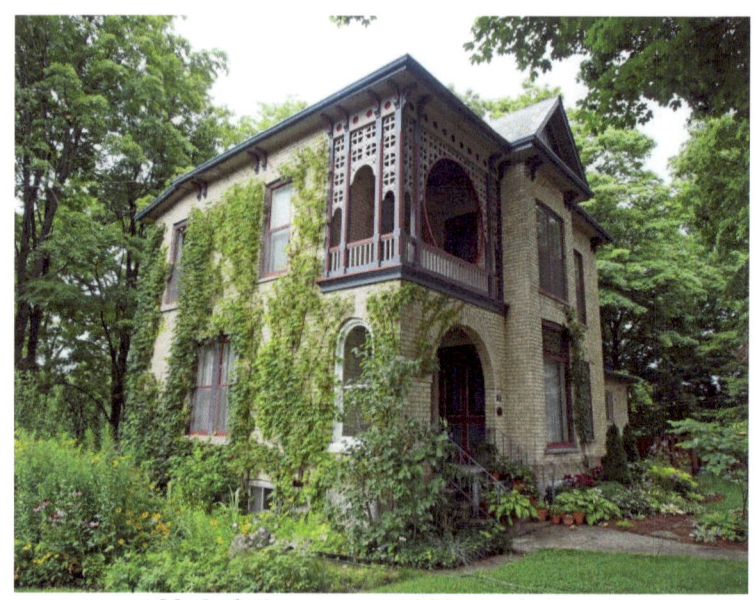

23 Oak Street – c. 1889 - Italianate

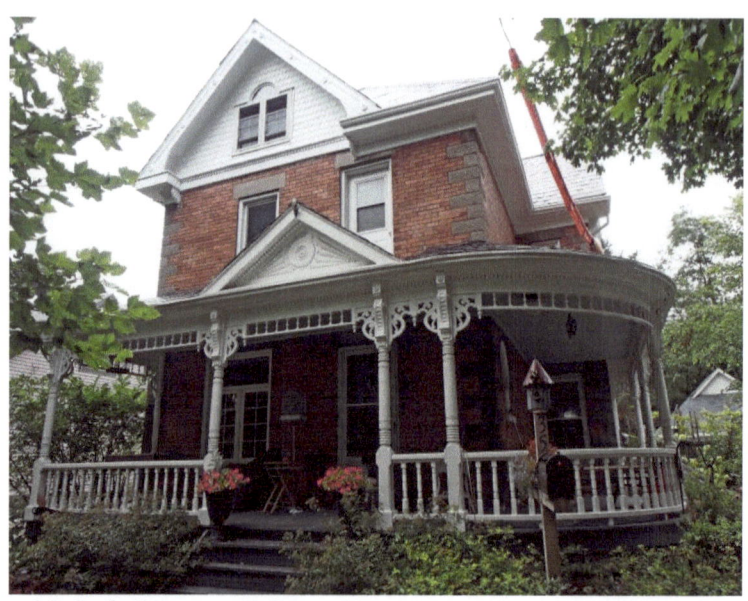

35 Oak Street – Edwardian, wraparound verandah,
pediment with decorated tympanum, corner quoins

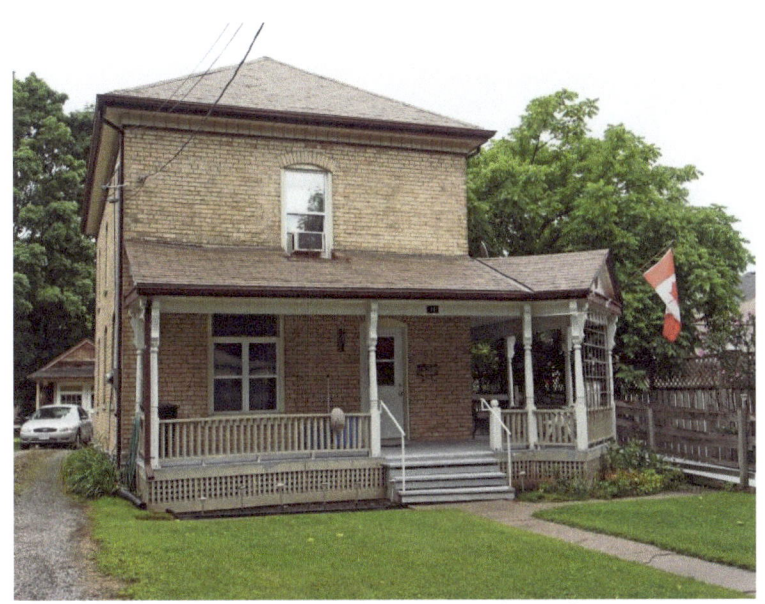

11 Oak Street – hipped roof

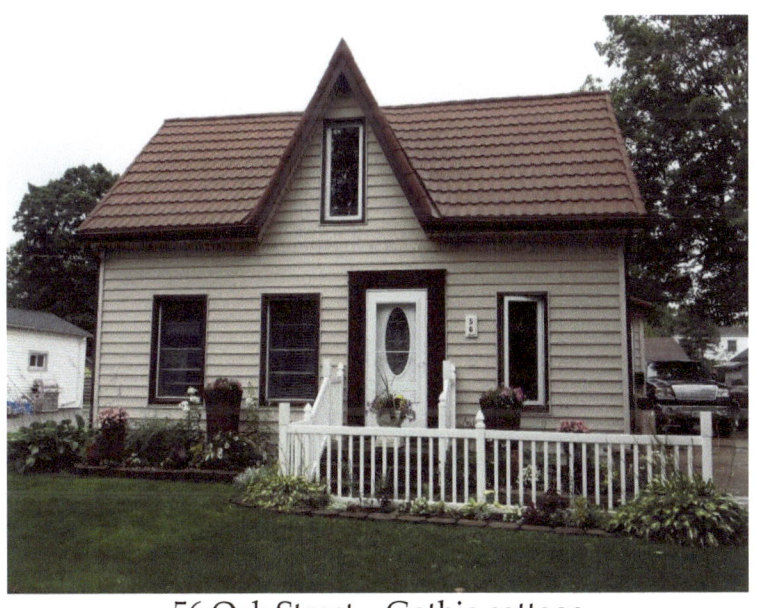

56 Oak Street – Gothic cottage

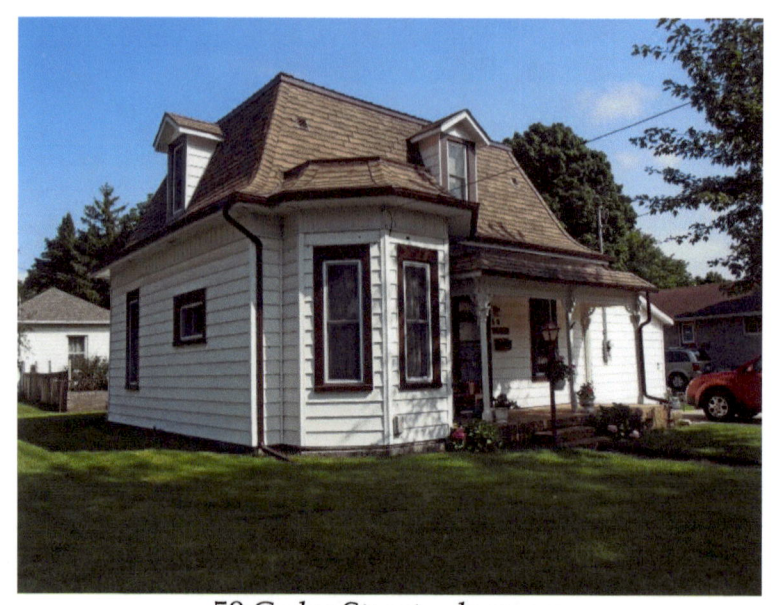

59 Cedar Street - dormers

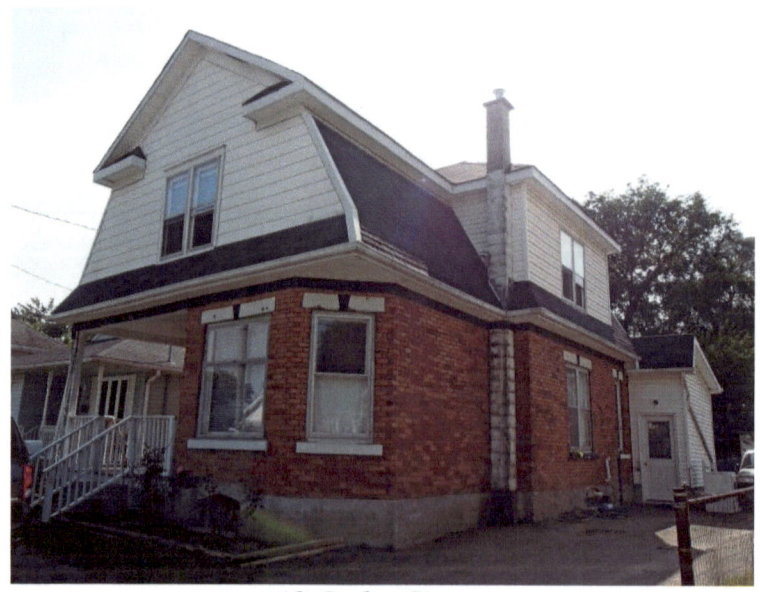

12 Cedar Street

Architectural Terms

Belvedere: (from the Italian "beautiful view") an architectural feature on a roof, in a garden or on a terrace that gives a beautiful view. Example: 30 South Street	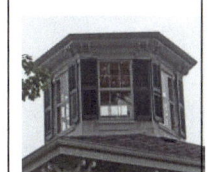
Brackets: a decorative or weight-bearing structural element which forms a right angle with one side against a wall and the other under a projecting surface such as an eave or roof. Example: 127 Talbot Street West	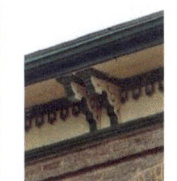
Buttress: a masonry structure built against or projecting from a wall which serves to support or reinforce the wall. In Canadian architecture, they are sometimes used for decoration. Example: 153 John Street South, Aylmer Baptist Church	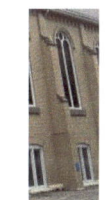
Capital: The uppermost finish or decoration on a column. An Ionic column has a small base, a thin elegant shaft, and a capital composed of volutes which are carved whirls or twists that take the form of a scroll. Example: 193 John S.	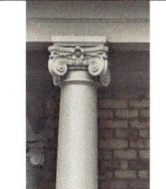
Cobblestone architecture: Refers to the use of cobblestones embedded in mortar as a method for erecting walls on houses and commercial buildings. Example: 127 Talbot Street West	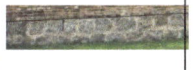

Cornice: originally the wooden overhang of the roof. With the use of stone, brick, iron and steel, the cornice is any projecting shelf at the top of a ceiling or roof. They can be very decorative. Example: 350 Talbot Street West	
Cornice Return: decorative element on the end of a gable. Example: St. John's Evangelical Lutheran Church	
Decorative Brickwork Example: 12 Harvey Street	
Dichromatic brickwork: the use of two colours of brick, tile or slate to decorate a façade. Trichromatic is the use of three colours. Example: 445 Talbot Street West	
Dormer: (French for "sleep") a gable end window that pierces through the plane of a sloping roof surface to create usable space in the top floor or attic of a building by adding headroom. Example: 383 Talbot Street West	
Fretwork: interlaced decorative design resembling a bracket Example: 452 Talbot Street West	
Gable: the triangular portion of a wall between the edges of a sloping roof. Example: 11 St. George Street	
Hipped Roof: a roof where all sides slope downwards to the walls with no gables. Example: 383 Talbot Street West	

Iron Cresting: A decorative ornament along the top of a roof. Iron cresting was popular in the Baroque era and also in Italianate, Victorian, Second Empire and Queen Anne styles of architecture. Example: 445 Talbot Street West	
Keystones and Voussoirs: a voussoir is a wedge-shaped element used in building an arch. A keystone is the central stone that locks all the stones into position, allowing the arch to bear weight. A keystone is often enlarged and embellished. Example: 167 John Street	
Lancet Window: a tall, narrow window with a pointed arch at its top. Example: 153 John Street South	
Mansard Roof: This style was popularized by Francois Mansart (1598-1666), an accomplished architect of the French Baroque period and especially fashionable during the Second French Empire (1852-1870). This roof is almost flat on the top section, with two slopes on each of its sides with the lower slope at a steeper angle than the upper and having dormer windows. Example: 445 Talbot Street West	
Palladian Window: a large window that is divided into three sections with the centre section larger than the two side sections and usually arched. Example: 31 Harvey Street	

Pediment: a triangular section above the horizontal structure (entablature), typically supported by columns. The inside of the triangle is called the tympanum. Example: 452 Talbot Street West	
Quoin: masonry blocks at the corner of a wall, often a decorative feature, usually larger or of a different colour than the rest of the wall. Example: Talbot Street West	
Turret: a small tower that projects from the wall of a building. Example: Talbot Street West	
Vergeboard and Finial: also called bargeboards – hang from the projecting end of a roof and are often elaborately carved and ornamented. **Finial:** ornament added to the top of a gable, pinnacle, canopy or spire – a Gothic element. Example: 136 Talbot Street West	
Window Hood: A **hood** is the piece found above window openings, usually of an ornate design, and covers the top third of the opening. Hoods are commonly placed above arched or curved openings on both windows and doors. Example: 10 Rutherford Avenue	

Building Styles

Edwardian, 1900-1930 – This style bridges the ornate and elaborate styles of the Victorian era and the simplified styles of the 20th century. Balanced facades, simple roof lines, dormer windows, large front porches, and smooth brick surfaces are its characteristics. Example: 452 Talbot Street	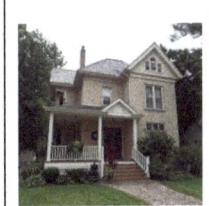
Georgian, before 1860 – This style began with the British King Georges in the 18th century. These buildings have balanced facades around a central door, medium-pitched gable roofs, and small paned windows. Example: 30 South Street	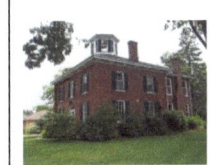
Gothic Revival, 1830-1890 – These decorative buildings have sharply-pitched gables with highly detailed vergeboards, pointed-arch window openings, and dichromatic brickwork. It is a common style in Ontario. Example: 20 South Street	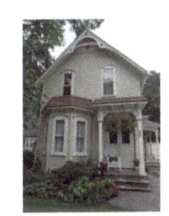
Italianate, 1850-1900 – It has wide-bracketed eaves, belvederes, wrap-around verandahs. Example: 383 Talbot Street West	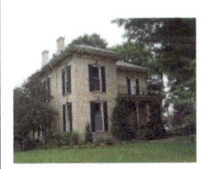

Queen Anne, 1885-1900 – This style is distinguished by an irregular outline featuring a combination of an offset tower, broad gables, projecting two-storey bays, verandahs, multi-sloped roofs, and tall, decorative chimneys. A mixture of brick and wood is common. Windows often have one large single-paned bottom sash and small panes in the upper sash. Example: Talbot Street West	
Regency Cottage, 1830-1860 – This style originated in England in 1815 and spread to Ontario later in the 19th century as British officers retired to Canada. It is a modest one-storey house with a low-pitched hip roof and has a symmetrical front façade. Example: 235 John Street South	
Romanesque Revival, 1880-1910 – This style hearkens back to medieval architecture of the 11th and 12th centuries with a heavy appearance, blocky towers and rounded arches. Example: 38 John Street South	
Second Empire, 1860-1880 – The mansard roof is the most noteworthy feature of this style and is evidence of the French origins. Projecting central towers and one or two-storey bays can also be present. Example: 445 Talbot Street West	
Tudor Revival – exposed timbers with stucco infill, multi-paned windows. Example: 24 South Street	